Spirituality
for an
Anxious Age
"Into Your Hands..."

Carol Spencer

1990

Spirit

+ San

Mr. 19.3

Spirituality
for an
Anxious Age
"Into Your Hands . . . "

Patrick J. Brennan

THE THOMAS MORE PRESS
Chicago, Illinois

Cloth ISBN 0-88347-178-7
Paper ISBN 0-88347-194-9

Contents

For my parents

INTRODUCTION

IN the last few years I have spoken in many different parts of the country. No matter where I have traveled, the themes that I speak of at retreats and renewals that seem to provoke the most interest and response are the areas of anxiety, stress, and depression. I have tried to systematically present in this book some of my reflections on a spiritual approach to emotional pain. These insights come from research, experiences in the counseling office, and my own struggles in personal, emotional and spiritual growth. I sincerely hope that they are of assistance to ministers and others whose role it is to heal the broken and hurting, as well as comforting to any who read them during a painful period in his or her life journey.

Patrick J. Brennan

CHAPTER ONE
Listening for Anxiety's Causes

IT happened again. Again this year I took time for a summer vacation, and there were several emotionally painful days and nights. Some days were filled with a restlessness mixed with guilt in the face of sudden inactivity. Some nights, at least into the wee hours of the morning, were a chaotic sea of insomnia mixed with confusing dreams. The admonition: "Aw, take a couple to slow yourself down!" does not work well with some of us. Alcohol's ability to depress the cortex but stimulate the cardiovascular system, seems to be acutely felt by some. The attempt to tranquilize with an outside agent sometimes is like gasoline on a fire. The blaze begins to burn with greater power, rather than diminish.

As I mentioned earlier, the phenomenon has struck before. Newton spoke of this phenomenon in the realm of physics when he said moving bodies seek to continue movement. To translate Newton's insight for our purposes, the moving body that we are concerned about is the *self*, a person. Difficulty in relaxing on a vacation for some of us is really the experience of seeing in microcosm the way we ordinarily are. The whirl and blur of daily activity anesthetize the human consciousness of some of the pain, the pain of contemporary stress-filled living. The absence of some of the scenery and props of daily busyness holds up to us in striking relief and contrast the craziness of the daily maze. For many, doing and achieving have become compulsions or addictions. To not have them to run to is somewhat akin to the drug addict's "going cold turkey" or the alcoholic's "drying out." To not have "what makes us tick" is somewhere on a continuum between discomfort and trauma.

The macrocosm is indeed contained and revealed in the microcosm. Anxious people are units of an increasingly anxious society. We could waste precious time and space in the philosophical "chicken and egg" dilemma. Which has come first—the age of anxiety (the culture of anxiety) or anxious people? Has the environment created the problem, that is, mass-produced anxious people? Or are some people born this way, or just like this? Suffice it to say individual personality type and the culture around us seem to do a wonderful "hand in glove" act. There is great complementarity between personality and culture. Dr. Theodore Issac Rubin expressed it well in his study, *Reconciliation: Inner Peace in An Age of Anxiety.* He said that we need no longer fantasize or make movies about the creature made by Frankenstein. Indeed, Frankenstein's monster lives in the anonymous, robotized, mechanical, and hurried lives that most of us live. We have become Frankenstein.

I wish to touch on the phenomena of anxiety, stress, and depression in this book. I would like to clarify terms at the outset. When I speak of anxiety, I am speaking of a "narrowing" of freedom, joy, consciousness, and spirit in life. The narrowing is rooted in fear. The fear can be of several points of origin:

fear of loss of control, fear of death, fear of abandonment, fear of meaninglessness. In anxiety, fear narrows life. The original German root, *angst*, means narrowing. Anxiety can be *acute*, manifesting itself in phobias, anxiety attacks and the like. It can also be chronic, of the "free-floating" genre. So many contemporary people suffer with this condition—a condition of being on guard, being alerted for danger, but not exactly knowing *why*. That which distinguishes *fear* from *anxiety* is specificity. Generally, one is afraid of someone or something. There is an objectivity to my fearful condition. The focus of anxiety is much more cluttered and diffuse. Most anxious people have lost touch with or have never been aware of exactly what they are afraid of.

Stress belongs to the anxiety family. It is chronic anxiety pushed to its extreme—to the point of taking a serious physiological toll. Stress reminds us of the *connectedness* of all of our parts and dimensions as human beings. The furnace of emotional energy cannot burn at an anxious, fever pitch for too long without becoming stress. Stress is anxiety beginning to wear out body parts: cardiovascular, gastrointestinal, cerebral. For anxious or stress-filled clients or parishioners, pastoral counseling or psychotherapy is best characterized by the words of the old song, *Getting to Know You*. In such cases the *you* that needs to be known is the *self*.

Anxiety is a fearful narrowing of life. *Stress* is a *physical—emotional* wearing down due to anxiety—often over the passage of time. That leads us to a final focus point: *depression*. As with anxiety and stress, there are forms of depression that are bio-chemically caused. Indeed, for some, chemical therapy is salvation, the only cure or amelioration for their painful condition. In discussing anxiety, stress, and depression I am not speaking of these conditions. Neither training nor experience has prepared me to discuss these aspects of emotional hurt. I mention them because their prevalence raises an important issue. Literally years of psychotherapy and much money can be saved if spiritual-emotional counseling is prefaced by or joined to a thorough physical examination. Mood swings, emotional narrowing, or seasons of gloom can be caused by physiological conditions that are easily tended to by medication.

In addressing depression, then, as with anxiety and stress, I am speaking of the type that is rooted in experience, environment, attitudes, or value conflicts. When I counsel someone whose symptoms are apparently expressive of depression, my mind usually races to two questions: What has she/he lost? What is she/he angry about? Depression is grief and/or anger, whose energy or passion has been turned inward, against the self. What confuses people about this interpretation of depression is that they begin to inventory their lives, looking for a major loss or reason for anger. But the loss or starting point for anger is in the person's perceptual system. The loss, hurt, or anger-producing factor can be related to the person's self image, bodily functions, employment situation, or position in the life cycle. Much depression-oriented loss or anger is indeed subtle, not adverted to, and unarticulated. We have a tendency to sweep things under the rug until we can no longer walk on the rug without tripping. Healing depression necessitates a naming of the objects or situations of loss and anger, and in the midst of the clouds, the rediscovery of rays of hope and reasons for living.

Our focus, then is on experience-oriented, environment-oriented, attitude and/or value-oriented anxiety, stress, and depression. I write about the three because I have found them to be remarkably related to each other and nurturing of each other.

Anxiety: Where Does the Stranger Come From?

Let us briefly examine the most significant theories regarding the origins and genesis of anxiety. Let us also limit our considerations to the modern, existentialist era. Close to two centuries ago, the father of modern existentialism, Soren Kierkegaard, connected a perceived increase in anxiety with the culture around him. Anxiety, Kierkegaard felt, was related to growing industrialization. He spoke almost like Rubin in seeing the mechanization of humanity as being also a source of its de-humanization and the cause of its increased anxiety.

Sigmund Freud's theories are widely known these days. For Freud, human beings were and are largely determined by instincts and passions. Anxiety is largely produced, in Freudian thinking, by the attempt at repressing the aggressive and sexual instincts and passions. Alfred Adler, whose theory we will consider more in depth later, broke with Freud over his deterministic view of humanity. For Adler, human beings were and are free beings. Rather than a symptom of repression, anxiety is rather symptomatic of human beings' struggle for significance. Adler felt that one of the basic human drives was for meaning or significance. That drive or need gets sidetracked quite often, or misdirected into a drive or need for power. To the degree one feels insignificant, meaningless, or indeed, powerless, one can begin to feel anxious.

Another Freudian, Carl Gustav Jung, expanded on Freud's notion of repression. For Jung, anxiety was symptomatic of the ego, or self, trying to quell or maintain the many chaotic forces of the unconscious. Jung's thoughts on the unconscious, in many ways, were more positive and expansive than those of Freud. For Jung, the unconscious was and is the realm of the symbolic, the collective memory and the unconscious of humankind. All of that is uncharted territory for many of us. We are reluctant and resist experiencing the contents of the unconscious. Our reluctance and resistance take the form of anxiety.

Flowing from the classical theories of Kierkegaard, Freud, Adler, and Jung, there have been many more contemporary theorists who have addressed the issue of anxiety. Interesting·among them are Karen Horney, Harry Stack Sullivan, and Otto Rank. Horney believed the etiology of anxiety was to be found in disturbed human relationships. In the life of the anxious person is the presence of unhappy, unsatisfying relationships, relationships that prevent an individual from achieving a value he/she holds to be of value.

Harry Stack Sullivan's theory speaks to the experience of many of us. Sullivan connected anxiety with the prospect of perceived or suspected disapproval. Sullivan speaks to those of us with "people pleaser tendencies." He interprets anxiety as a consequence of not pleasing, of incurring disapproval. This syndrome begins, Sullivan felt, in the mother-child relationship.

Otto Rank's theory about anxiety is perhaps the most inclusive and representative of reality. Rank saw anxiety as necessarily involved in each person's process of individuation. One way of summarizing Rank's thoughts is this: we get anxious because we are afraid to live and afraid to die. Indeed, life and death are the two major life issues we all must face, and we must face them alone, individually. Facing life and death causes anxiety.

Herbert Freudenberger has further specified the dynamics of anxiety in a recent study *Situational Anxiety*. Freudenberger feels that all of us suffer from anxiety in varying degrees. *Situational anxiety* in Freudenberger's thinking refers to how specific things in day-to-day living act as catalysts for unpleasant, uncomfortable, and often unwanted feelings. Freudenberger postulates that the catalytic dynamic results from unsolved issues, experiences, or relationships in the past. Freudenberger categorizes types of situational anxiety. Among his categories are: sexual anxiety (discomfort over one's own sexual feelings, one's own attractiveness, or sexual performance), aloneness anxiety (late afternoon anxiety or fear of the night, insomnia or fear of not being

able to sleep), anxiety over public aloneness (agoraphobia or fear of open spaces with many people),
anxiety over being late, party anxiety, birthday anxiety, doctor anxiety, and on and on.

In a profound book, *Christotherapy II* (companion
to *Christotherapy I*) Bernard Tyrrell addresses a
theme of this book, no matter what the etiology of
anxiety. Tyrrell speaks of the need to educate the
feeling of fear. Fear, he would agree with Adler, is
the result of *learned* dysfunctional approaches to life.
Growth from fear involves educating impoverished,
painful ways of approaching life. Tyrrell speaks of a
movement from diseased fear responses to highly
spiritualized responses to life. Enslaving, crippling,
neurotic fear, Tyrrell writes, can become a kind of
holy, reverential fear; fear related to the self can also
sensitize one to greater empathy with the fearfulness
of others. Key to the education of fear is the penetration of learned, irrational fear responses to life with
attitudes rooted in trust in life and courage for life.

Tyrrell has a catch phrase that I intentionally
pause on, for it expresses a keen, though nonetheless
paradoxical insight into the healing of anxiety. There
can be no education of fear, or conversion therapy as
Aidan Kavanaugh speaks of, without the *will to
discomfort*. I cannot grow from fear and anxiety if I
am unwilling to put myself in often uncomfortable
situations and settings which may become crucibles
and thresholds where new responses to life other
than my fear can be learned. The anxiety-prone person has conditioned resistance to such new "firing-
line positions" in which new "fear-less" responses

might be learned. Often, discernment as to what such learning situations might even be necessitate the presence of a therapeutic or spiritual friend or companion who can help us decide on which are the intra- and inter-personal battles that we need to choose to create an environment for growth. Tyrrell's evocative phrase, "the will to discomfort," will be explored in different ways later in the book. Growth from anxiety necessitates decisions which in effect "spit in the soup" of our neuroses and neurotic constructs.

A noteworthy entry in the field of literature on anxiety is David Sheehan's book, *The Anxiety Disease*. Sheehan feels that for some *dysfunctional anxiety* often has three parallel roots. Notice that included here is the term *dysfunctional anxiety*, for there are other forms of anxiety that are normal, appropriate to a stimulus or situation and, in fact, stimulating to growth. Some artists, athletes and scholars would not produce without some precipitating anxiety. Dysfunctional anxiety is that which "gets in the way" of relatively happy, peaceful living and relationships.

The three parallel and simultaneously present causes of dysfunctional anxiety in some people, in Sheehan's research are: 1) a *physical disorder* (a neurobiological problem); 2) *psychological conditioning* (learned fear responses to one's environment or inner reality); 3) an actual situation or environment that is anxiety producing. The "anxiety disease" progresses through seven stages according to Sheehan: 1) spells of free-floating anxiety; 2) panic attacks; 3) hypochondriasis, or preoccupation with disease; 4) phobia; 5) fear of people's judgments and reactions; 6) agoraphobia, or extensive fear of people or situations; and 7) a kind of paralysis or acute anxiety that is wedded to depression.

In Sheehan's thought, close scrutiny needs to be paid with such people, to all three of the contributing causes. Because the causes come from a three-fold cluster, often such people need drug or chemical therapy joined to psychotherapy that challenges the learned conditioning, plus forms of behavior modification and environmental de-sensitization.

Listening in the Age and Culture of Anxiety

In preparing couples for marriage, I often speak of the commandments of the culture which militate against the intimacy that they seek. The cultural commandments could be summarized as: 1) *Business:* We are conditioned to find self-worth in activity, and a lack of self-worth in inactivity or self-reflection; 2) *My agenda:* In a holdover pattern from the seventies, we remain compulsive about what we want, need or feel we must be or do. My *agenda-ism* of course flies in the face of the emotional and spiritual challenges of *tending to other's agenda* or together forming *our agenda;* 3) *It-ism:* What are the criteria for success in our age? Certainly they are related to the accumulation of things. I thought *thing-orientation,* or *it-ism* was a phenomenon unique to white middle-class culture until I began working and consulting with people and ministers in the inner city of Chicago. While the contextual situations or environments in such neighborhoods are hardly those of affluence, there is nonetheless an imperative toward affluence. Making it is somehow tied up with the acquisition of things that speak of success. Center city people certainly want to get to the fringe of the city or suburbia, where the *its*, the *things* speak of having arrived; 4) *Competition:* If there is a generic golden calf in our culture, it is *success*. If there is any way to get to "the carrot" of success, it is to live with an attitude of *competition*. Adlerian psychotherapy speaks of cooperation as one of the hallmarks of healthy living. The co-operative person is not so much anxious to stand out or stand apart as he/she is to "fit in," become part of the whole, contribute to the general well-being. Competition does not permit co-operation.

Busyness, my agenda, it-ism, and *competition* are catch-phrases or generic terms that attempt to capture the tone of the age of anxiety. I have paused on them to highlight a crucial point. The attitudes and values represented by these umbrella terms collide with people experiencing intimacy with each other. More specific to our concerns, these and other attitudes block true intimacy with one's self. The absence of intimacy with one's self is at the root of anxiety, stress, and depression. Symptoms of anxiety arise when we are not in touch, when we are not making time to understand—*when we are not listening*. I cannot be intimate with someone whom I love if I am unwilling to listen to that person. Neither can I be intimate, or *congruent with myself* (as Carl Rogers speaks of it), if I am unwilling to begin listening to myself.

Case Studies in the Problem of Listening to Self

CAROL: Carol came to see me recently. She is an attractive young woman, completing her undergraduate studies in preparation for a career of nursing. Carol has always been a low-keyed, pleasing type of person. She has always personally valued her physical abilities and her natural skills in athletics. Those skills do not do much, however, in the halls and classrooms of nursing preparation. To throw further coal on the fire, Carol has developed her first significant emotional-sexual relationship in her first months on campus. Her male friend does much to contribute to her ego-strength, self-image, and feelings of attractiveness; yet he also makes demands, demands of emotional energy and mutuality. The demands of professionalism and a deep relationship do not have a lot of resonance with Carol's previously defined simplistic worldview and self concept. She has begun to develop symptoms—symptoms of anxiety and distress. She cries frequently and has become indecisive. Most frightening for her, she has begun to fear for her own sanity. She has developed that perhaps most painful of anxiety indicators—the fear of losing one's mind, the fear of losing control.

In developing a counseling relationship with Carol, the first thing that I tried to help her learn is the skill of listening to herself. A counselor who greatly influenced my life used to anger me when I went to see him when I was Carol's age. I would present my fears, conflicts, phobias, and relational difficulties. After listening to them, he would almost dismiss them and challenge me: "OK, let's get beyond the symptoms to what is really bothering you." I would get angry at him for apparently minimizing the pain of what I was experiencing. After many sessions, I caught on to the counselor's wisdom. He was trying to teach me to listen—listen beyond the level of the external to what was happening within me, to what, in effect, I was saying to myself and to life. The blur of my life had deafened me to what was inside. His lesson on the need to listen to self has been a perduring one for me.

PHIL: Carol and Phil's stories lend support to my conviction that young adults pass through what is perhaps one of the most spiritual of life's seasons. Both questions of identity and intimacy are being wrestled with, especially in the 18 to 25 age bracket. Phil was a middle child carrying within himself some of the baggage that state in life presents, among them, *self-doubt*. Phil's *self-doubt* was influenced by the sudden death of a brother in an early morning car accident on a suburban highway. The self-doubt and the rage about his brother's death were introjected. At the time of requesting some time with me, Phil was experiencing bouts of insomnia, anxiety attacks that woke him in the middle of the night, and fears of "losing control" in his college classroom. Phil had developed symptoms—disguised, symbolic expressions of the turmoil within. His night fears reflected a fearfulness about himself relative to life in general; the night hours revealed his ultimate "aloneness" to him. His fears about loss of control in a social context (i.e., the classroom) spoke of a deep rage within—against life, against those from whom he presumed negative judgment, against his brother's death.

Pastoral counseling took the form of trying to listen beyond the symtoms—to the anger, rage, and hurt. Phil, of course, had to get to the feelings encased in the symptoms. While I could intuit some of them, I could not impose my interpretation. As he heard them, and named them, he could begin to own them and manage them better. Anxiety is so often the situation of unattended to, unnamed feelings swirling about below the level of consciousness.

NELL: Nell is a twenty-seven-year-old who grew up in an Americanized version of Irish Catholicism. She, her parents, brothers, and sisters were raised in Ireland. They came to America about a decade ago in the hope of economic advancement. Nell's mother is a dominant force in the family—to the point that one of the main thrusts of Nell's life vision has been to please her mother. Just exactly what pleases Nell's mother is never quite clear. Nell's crisis is a collision between her own emerging young-adult needs, and the restrictions she feels concerning pleasing her mother. Her presenting symptoms are anxiety oriented, manifesting themselves in periods of undefined fear and panic.

Nell's conversations with me also hinted at another undercurrent in her life. She would vaguely hint at loneliness, and relationships that once were significant but now were over. After several sessions which built up trust, she was able to share her truth with me. A significant relationship that she had with a young male friend had ended because of the bizarre behavior connected with her anxiety attacks. Nell enfleshes an insight Adler had into anxiety and other emotional reactions: that we indeed use our emotions for a purpose. Nell's purpose was escape. She desperately wanted a relationship with her boyfriend; yet the relationship threatened her equanimity with her mother. Her anxiety symptoms warded off the threatening male. Because they were tied in with an emotional condition, she was able to convince herself that "things were happening to her" over which she had no control. In that approach, she was also able to rid herself of responsibility for the flow of her own life. Her life was happening to her; she was not *doing* her life.

But part of Nell's emotional pain was repressed anger, anger at the familial situation that she allowed to dictate to her. Specifically, she was quite angry, indeed in a grief reaction at the loss of a young man whom her emerging adult self desired.

It was so easy for Nell to claim craziness. In fact, underneath all those symptoms of craziness were glaring needs and feelings not being attended to. Emotional realities swept under the carpet eventually trip those who have been trying to conceal them. The beginning of Nell's healing process was learning how to do deep listening within herself, and then naming what was within.

JOHN: Lest the reader begin to feel this is a book on young-adult crises, let us switch the focus to a mid-lifer. John is forty-one years old. For years he has been dissatisfied with marriage, having married a woman much more aggressive and assertive than he. Some years ago, she began a process of self-improvement that included professionalization in an area of life she had been long interested in. At that point in their marriage, some eight years ago, he felt his first wave of discomfort with the relationship. That discomfort led to a growing verbal and physical exchange of hostility between the two of them. He just knew that he was unhappy. He did not know why; nor did he see or name the rage boiling from within him.

John came to me recently at the request of his wife. Their problem: he no longer loved her. He was in fact attracted to another woman, one he worked with. Several months of discussions with John led him to see how much he did not want to look or listen within. What he especially could not listen to was a very strong voice that was announcing that his marriage was ended—through. He no longer loved his wife. In fact, he was terribly angry at his wife. She was for him a symptom of loss—loss of youth, hope, and dreams. She was in fact unfaithful to him—in his perception—going all the way back to when she began her career, and left him in her dust. Naming his anger and feelings of loss over the years cleared the air for decisions about the future.

Carol, Phil, John; any helper could tell similar stories of encountering people in conflict—people looking for someone to help clarify the maze of their lives. Eugene Gendlin, in his book, *Focusing*, soberly reminds therapists and counselors of the essential role that we play in people's lives. We help people who have lost focus, to focus. If the counselor is indeed interested in helping, he/she should be most interested in imparting to the person in conflict the ability to focus, to listen. The counselor is someone trying to work himself/herself out of a job by transferring to the client or person in need the skills for listening.

Learning to Listen

Gendlin's exciting proposition is that the therapeutic strategies of the professional helper can be learned by the ordinary person. What does a helper do for someone who comes seeking assistance or guidance? He/she creates a hospitable, welcoming environment, an environment that suggests to the person seeking help that he/she can share openly and honestly and do that with someone who will sensitively listen. That therapeutic-listening environment allows a person to let his/her mind run, leading to a number of verbalizations regarding thoughts and feelings that hitherto had perhaps been not shared.

A third stage in the therapeutic process is to move toward precision in naming those thoughts and feelings. Feelings especially need to be accurately named. Am I feeling threatened, hurt, tired, angry, jealous, sexual—whatever. Naming feelings provides a kind of liberation, a release. Gendlin says that a person needs to go back then and repeat the process, to better assure accuracy in the naming process.

I heard a comparison once between the human personality and the automobile. If an automobile that we are driving begins to make noises, we usually either look under the hood, or take the vehicle to someone who can interpret the extraneous noises. The personality demands the same sensitivity, but we rarely give it to ourselves. Noises are constantly coming "from under the hood" but we ignore them. Gendlin's methodology demands that we "pick up the hood" not only of our cars but of ourselves.

Listening and naming have become important parts of my spiritual journey. I have learned to make time to listen at all sorts of different times: before an important event when my heart begins to mysteriously beat with intensity; as I drive from meeting to meeting; when I feel vague waves of something being wrong; at moments of leisure when paradoxically I cannot relax when I am supposed to; and also when I am feeling quite stable and complacent. I feel that being "in touch" is not just a luxury for when I feel emotional pain, but something that should be a staple part of my daily emotional-spiritual life.

Listening to self requires a discipline. The discipline requires a commitment to time that will be spent in "looking under the hood." The discipline demands a relentless honesty that seeks to get at the truth of the feeling, no matter what the feeling is. For me, the discipline necessitates an obvious "God" dimension. As I uncover who I am, I do it not just with and for myself. I do it with the Lord. Deep listening provides me with material for prayer and spiritual growth. Prayer has become for me less a task I must perform and more a time when I can be totally who I am in the presence of the ultimate other—the Lord. As I uncover who I am and what is going on within me, as I feel the freedom to be totally who I am in the Presence of the Lord, I can also begin to rehearse for life—to prayerfully prepare to be a disciple of the Lord in the course of my tasks and relationships during the day.

William Glasser, writing some years ago in *Positive Addictions*, recommended that contemporary Americans join twenty minutes of meditation to other daily life-giving, life-restoring disciplines. What this daily diet will look like needs to be designed by each unique person. Such a discipline of meditation and positive addicitions are deliberate steps to counter the malignant numbness brought on by living according to the compulsions of *busyness, my agenda, it-ism,* and *competition.*

A technique that can be helpful in the process of listening toward spiritual wholeness is journaling. Writing newly discovered thoughts and feelings down—in a stream of consciousness, poetry, stories, or prayers—is a way of incarnating, enfleshing the mystery of "self with God" unfolding within.

Herbert Freudenberger, mentioned earlier, published another recent study entitled *Burn-out*. In it, he analyzes some of the classic symptoms of a person who is emotionally and spiritually drained from the routines of life. Among the symptoms are increased physical (psychosomatic) complaints, feelings of being unappreciated, sexual dysfunctioning, and drug or alcohol abuse. Freudenberger says a typical response to burn-out symptoms is to increase activity and to deny what is happening within. Actually, Freudenberger says, only a new spirit of inner directedness and a new openness to intimacy can revive our drooping spirits. It is inner directedness and intimacy that are the key ingredients of the spiritual strategy suggested in this book. The inner-directedness and intimacy begin with the self and unfold increasingly to integrate significant others and God.

Listening for God

Listening is indeed a basic step in self understanding. Listening leads to naming feelings and thoughts. Naming helps me toward insight or understanding why I feel or think the way I do. The Judaeo-Christian tradition believes in a God who continuously is communicating with his people. We call this communication "revelation." While we believe God's self-revelation reached completion in the *Word made Flesh*, Jesus: we also believe that full revelation is re-echoing in our own day. The Word made Flesh through Jesus is mysteriously present and alive in our own day. That Word is being spoken to us often in our own deep memory, in our conscience, in our unconscious, in our imagination, in our own thoughts and feelings. God's Word takes on a variety of shapes and forms. Sometimes we receive a word of challenge. At other times the word is comforting. Still other times the word is indicting. Often, the word is healing and reconciling.

The Word of God is spoken to us each day as really as it was to the great heroes and heroines of Scripture. In this age of *hurry sickness*, we have dulled our perceptive abilities. The "Incarnation intuition," that God is alive and communicating in the human story, is often blocked in our culture. The Word goes ignored, or unheard. The person of faith who is trying to become a deep listener gradually realizes that one cannot seriously listen to self without beginning to listen to God also.

Listening to Others

Part of the anxiety of our age can be attributed to the isolation many of us live in. Work, expectations and pressures can isolate us from our fellow human beings. In many parts of the country the experience of close-knit families living in equally close-knit neighborhoods is now a memory. Not only do we fail to listen to ourselves and to God, often we neglect to listen to each other. The astronomical rise in the number of people regularly visiting psychotherapists and counselors is one of the indicators that people indeed need someone who will listen to them. The work of Thomas Gordon in *Parent Effectiveness Training* and *Teacher Effectiveness Training* challenged parents in recent years to see that many discipline problems could be alleviated if the child were sure that he or she were being listened to. Other researchers have shown listening to be the key to improving many different kinds of relationships, from marital to work.

Listening is one of the key behaviors of the Kingdom. While Jesus is often portrayed in the gospels as speaking, he also is portrayed as *being with* others. Listening is a sign of *hospitality,* or being willing to enter the pain and stories of another person. Listening requires a real discipline or asceticism on the part of the listener. That discipline involves letting go of my agenda, my busyness, my compulsions to attend to another. In the 24th chapter of *Luke,* Jesus spends significant time in the journey to Emmaus *being with* the other two travelers, and asking questions that help the two reveal who they are. He saves his input for later. In following a process of presence, listening, and later speaking to them, Jesus facilitates something in them. They "come to recognize" him. The experience of "coming to recognize" is the experience of insight, or learning in its purest form. Whether we are trying to grow in insight into ourselves, or to help another gain insight, listening is an important preliminary behavior. The lesson of Emmaus is that presence and listening create an environment wherein we can "come to see."

CHAPTER TWO
Insights, Decisions, and Changed Behavior

I THINK one of the reasons we avoid listening is that it leads us to insight. Insight, in turn, leads to a situation of unrest in which we are almost "nagged" toward new decisions. The nagging comes from ourselves and the Lord. It is the best self beckoning or inviting the status quo self. It is the Spirit of God prompting and encouraging us. So often people in emotional pain see no way out, no exit.

The "no exit" experience speaks of how anxiety and stress are often connected with depression. Depression is a loaded topic to deal with, for there is no one, united syndrome that constitutes depression. Depression, rather, is an umbrella term that covers a number of syndromes. In this brief commentary on depression, I will not be dealing with depression as it manifests itself in grief over the death of a loved one. Neither will I be speaking of forms of depression that are bio-chemically induced. This latter form of depression points to the necessity, in most cases of depression, to begin with a complete physical examination. That would rather quickly determine any biological causality for depression.

On Depression and Resignation

In the first chapter, I suggested three related notions that have helped me understand depression.

The three are: *anger, loss,* and *lacking.* In many depressed people, a low grade anger is seething right
below the surface of things. The anger is introjected
upon the self, rather than being focused on the proper object or person. At times, the anger is connected
with the *no exit* phenomenon, the feeling that a person is without options in terms of his or her future.
Sometimes related to the feeling of anger is the felt
experience of *loss.* Many sad or depressed people
feel that they have lost something quite integral to
their lives. The loss can be quite subtle: youth,
possibilities, appearance, prestige, etc. Finally, sad,
depressed people often have "lacking" feelings. Relative to life's tasks, they perceive themselves as lacking in necessary qualities, abilities, or opportunities
to be who they are meant to be. Whether we are trying to understand ourselves or minister to another,
three questions are helpful in trying to pinpoint sadness or depression: "What am I mad about? What
have I lost? What do I see myself as lacking?"

The anger-loss-lacking pattern can be free-standing
of itself. In other words, depression can be an independent entity. But frequently it is related to other
phenomena, namely anxiety or stress. When related to
anxiety or stress, depression frequently casts a tone or
mood over the person: "I am in this emotional situation, and I have no way to get out." Anxious-depressed people frequently grow oblivious to a God-
given ability we all have: the ability to make *decisions.*

In previous decades of Christianity, *resignation
spirituality* was encouraged. Resignation spirituality
was and is deceptive. When described it sounds

somewhat akin to spiritual surrender, which is so crucial for true conversion. Surrender is a letting go, a releasing into a power or force that is more than the self, and which contains within itself creative, transforming power. Resignation contains some of the tone of surrender. The major difference between resignation and surrender is one of intentionality. In a stance of surrender, I fully intend to let go of some of my ego or will to better experience communion with a higher power. Resignation, on the other hand, is a stance of apathy or boredom. It is the assuming of a helpless or hopeless stance toward life. It is the stagnation which Erik Erikson warned adults about. Frequently, it is a stance that can be used to avoid growth. Implicit in resignation spirituality is a potentially dangerous outlook on God: he is the source of any good, but also any misfortune that befalls me. Resignation spirituality fosters an unhealthy dependence on God that says, in effect, we have nothing to say about how our lives unfold.

Nothing could be further from the truth. Though life contains an untold number of turns in the road and "life accidents," which we will discuss later, we exist in a co-operative relationship with the Lord. We do, indeed, co-create with him. People who have begun to appropriate the spirituality of Jesus know that *covenant* is a dialogical reality. God has offered himself to us. He has decided for us; he has decided to be our God. He in turn invites us to decide in response, decide to be his people. The essence of our covenant response to God is this: since I have been gifted with life, I decide to be responsible with the gift, to do my best to be the self God made me to be, to co-operate in finding the unique spiritual direction my life should take. *Covenanting* or *deciding* for life and God happens in at least two ways in daily life. There are major covenant moments in our lives in which we struggle to re-orient the major direction of our lives. Then there are also less emotionally charged moments, when the major direction chosen earlier in life is decided again, and motivation and intentionality is purified.

A major covenanting period in my life was in my early twenties, when I had to come to grips with a great amount of anxiety and stress present in my young-adult life. Listening to myself and others listening to me facilitated insight into my situation, insight that some of my pain was not being inflicted on me, but rather that I was causing much of it myself by my own attitudes toward self, others, life, and God. I entered a major covenanting period in my life, wherein I vowed to the Lord to transform some of the pain that I brought on myself. There was great insight and truth in that covenanting period. Since then, I've had many times of re-covenanting in which I try again to commit myself to that wholeness and responsible living. The core of all such covenants of growth, be they major or minor ones, is decision-making. I worked with a young man in high school recently who hung a banner in his room to remind himself of the creative ability he had in his own life. The banner read: "You can, if you think you can." While the adolescent was trying to shore himself up for basketball tryouts and other adolescent crises of growth, his banner expressed a lot of truth about the nature of growth for all ages. People grow if they want to and if they decide to.

Decisions About What?

We are non-reflectively making decisions all of the time. The process is going on even in the life of the infant. The psychologist, Alfred Adler, talked about this years ago in his concept of *lifestyle*. Very early in life, Adler suggested, all of us begin to construct a lifestyle, or a system of *rules* that we operate by in life and *roles* that we play in life. The lifestyle is freely chosen and constructed. Family, early experiences, one's ordinal position in the family and other such factors influence the lifestyle, but the lifestyle is essentially freely chosen. In emphasizing the freedom and decision-making ability of the individual, Adler began a process of divorce from Freud, of whom Adler was originally a disciple. Freud, of course, saw the human person as determined, pushed, and pulled by unconscious forces both around and within.

The rules and roles, or the lifestyle, that we decide for in a step by step way throughout life, touch on the most simple yet most complex issues of what it means to be a human being. These issues include:

–Who am I? What do I really think and feel about myself?
–What is my outlook on life? How do I perceive life? What are my attitudes toward the world around me?
–What are people like? What do people want or

expect from me? What do I have to offer in a
relationship?
–Who loves me? Am I lovable? How do I get
love?
–Who should I be and become?
–What are the *musts, oughts, shoulds,* and *have
tos* that propel me into activity?

As we ask ourselves those questions, again often in
a preconscious, unarticulated, intuitive sort of way,
we make decisions in a similar fashion, that answer
the questions, and begin to mold and shape life. Unfortunately, there is present in most of our rules and
roles both strength and weakness, both truth and
mistaken notions. One's decisions and answers to
life questions can contain thoughts and attitudes that
are far from objective truth about the self, the world,
life, relationships, and life's imperatives. One of the
threads running through this study of spirituality
and emotional pain is my belief that we cause a great
deal of our own emotional pain by the life decisions,
often non-reflectively reached and lived out, that we
ourselves have chosen.

The hope in this last statement is this: once we
have *listened* and gained *insight* into some of our
mistaken notions we are free and capable to re-
decide for healthier and happier living. We are not
victims and martyrs. To a large degree we are in the
driver's seat of our own lives. Early models of psychotherapy stress a disease approach to emotional
distress. If I have a disease concept of emotional
pain, then I can see myself as a piece in a game in

which someone else is calling the shots. The better approach to emotional problems and helping people is an educational model. In an educational approach, the task of both the person in pain and the helper is to learn. The focus of learning is the person's network of experiences, perceptions, and decisions that may have contributed to his/her emotional conflict. The educational model seeks to find new decisions and new behavior patterns that might contribute to a more peaceful way of life.

The Dream and Intentionality

Decision-making takes a unique form in the adult years. Early in adulthood, we begin to form "the dream," or the ideal shape and form that our lives will take. The dream flows from and is congruent with the lifestyle, or whole thrust of one's life. Just as the lifestyle can be flawed with mistaken notions, or privatized logic, so also the dream (which involves the public persona one presents to the world, career and vocational choices, socio-economic status, and so forth) can lead an individual away from true self-actualization. The dream, while it is the source of motivation for daily behavior, can in fact be at the root of self-alienation.

Consider the mid-life gentleman who reported in a counseling situation recently that he literally hates his job. The buildup of resentment within him is being repressed, and causing depression-like symptoms. The obvious, most facile advice is to seek new employment, perhaps even a different line of work that might be more in line with his interests and personality. But he resists even the slightest mention of such a development. He needs that job to maintain his image, his style of living, his family's expectations for comfort. His dream—that of the successful business executive—is getting in the way of his happiness. The dream has become alienating.

In his classic *Love and Will*, Rollo May wrote of the importance of intentionality in emotional health. He spoke of the person with emotional problems as a person whose intentionality is confused. Intentionality refers to the whole direction of a person's life, his/her ambitions, goals, and life plan. The dream is the energy source for intentionality. Frequently, anxiety, stress, depression, or other painful emotional states is the result of misguided or diffuse intentionality. In his own symbolic way, Jesus referred to intentionality when he spoke of the need for one master in a person's life.

Synthesis on Decision-Making

In summary, we are more in charge of our own destinies than we think we are. To forget that is to engage in a self-deception that life just happens to us. Some of life does happen. But a significant portion we arrange. To what degree do we arrange our own pain by deciding on and continuing to live out of faulty values, attitudes, and thought patterns about self, others, life, and God? When we get serious about our own destinies, we begin to get serious about the power we have to make life decisions. There is a dawning in most adult lives, which I referred to at the outset of this chapter. That period I call the experience of "covenanting" with God for growth. We wake up at such a time to the shape and direction of our lives. We become aware of some of the things we need to do to be our best selves, the self God apparently is calling us to be and become. In a significant way we decide for growth, asking God's help in all the struggles involved in the process of growth. That initial covenant, for some made in the young-adult years of our lives, for others at some other life stage, needs re-enforcement. At many different stages of life, decisions of less magnitude are needed to continue on the road of wellness and wholeness.

In the *Varieties of Religious Experience*, William James spoke of two types of religious conversion—conversion of surrender and volitional conversion. While I will speak in depth of conversion later in the book, his distinctions are helpful at this point. Volitional conversion is James's term for "a choice or decision for growth," in this case spiritual growth. In volitional conversion, a person literally takes his or her life in hand and decides to change it. The person sees the self in an imaginary mirror, and is in a state of unrest because what he or she perceives is not the self that could be. Many people speak of an inner nagging that is relentless until a decision is made to direct one's energies toward that best self. I believe that "inner nagging" can indeed be interpreted sometimes as the call of God, or the promptings of the Holy Spirit—calling us to leave the comfortable distortion of the status quo of our lives—to move to the desert. In the desert, we confront our demons, and are comforted by God's Spirit. But we rarely leave a desert experience unchanged.

Listening, Insights, and Decisions That Lead to Behavior Change

One of the weaknesses of the psychotherapies that might be labeled "insight" therapies is that they lead people to a great understanding of themselves, but not necessarily to any strategies concerning how to change their lot in life. There is some profit in knowing why we are anxious, stress-filled, or depressed. But there is even more profit in discovering ways in which we can transform negative energies into positive ones. The inadequacy of the insight therapies led to the popularity of the behavior, or behavior modification therapies. The behavior therapies do not place a very high valence on understanding or insight, or listening to self. Whether "contracting" with a child whose behavior is inappropriate in the classroom, to "placing a new behavior tape" in an adult's consciousness, behaviorists are technicians whose goal it is to re-program behavior.

Both insight and behavior therapists have a piece of the truth, and the great truth is found in an integration of their approaches. The listening person, gaining insight into self, is motivated to make decisions about new directions for the self. Those new directions ought to lead to new behavior, new ways of doing things. Put another way, change of attitudes and change of behavior can become mutually re-enforcing energies. To act in a new way supports attempts at changing one's heart. On the other hand, changing my heart provides the energy that is needed to engage in real behavior change.

Behavior change is indeed the most difficult part of any therapeutic process. As my counselor-spiritual director often says to me, "Brennan, you're insightful into your own problems. You've become a good listener to your own thoughts and feelings, lifestyle and dreams. But you still do not like to change things. You even allow painful situations to go on and on." He is right. The hardest thing for me in my own passage from anxiety to trust and peace is to change behavior. Behavior change has to become part of the covenant package between myself and the Lord. As I make decisions about changing my interior life, I know now I have to build into the covenant specific steps I am also going to take to change my behavior.

Perhaps you are familiar with the slogan "love is a decision," so popular in the Marriage Encounter Movement. It is a way of articulating the importance of behavior, though the reference to behavior is elliptical in the slogan. What is being said in the slogan is, in essence: "There are some days you will not feel love toward your spouse, but on those days you must remember that you made a decision: to actively love your spouse daily." On days spouses do not feel like loving, they still need to love. The act of loving eventually melts their hearts. Again, attitude and behavior change are mutually re-enforcing.

For me, it is important to do decision-making about

the future of my life and to map out behavior changes for myself in tandem, the one mirroring the other. I again cannot stress enough the importance of the journal, not only as a tool for listening and insight, or self-probing, but also for decision-making and behavior mapping, or self-directing. In other words, covenanting, whether it be of the magnitude of major life changes, or daily attempts at growth, can be articulated and charted in the journal. The journal has the ability to get what is inside of us outside of us. It helps us to take the amorphous and nebulous within us and make it concrete, so that we can look at it, talk about it, pray about it, or share it with a trusted other. Though the journal is not for everyone, it certainly has been a remarkable tool for many of us concerned about emotional-spiritual growth. Through it, we can even personally forgive persons and situations in the past, present, or future that are a source of stress or hurt for us. Through journaling, we are provided with the release of catharsis (emotional purging), ventilation (sharing of thoughts and convictions) and sometimes abreaction (vicarious re-living of an event).

Behavior Change and "As If" Days

Most counselors or helpers, indeed most folks in counseling or therapy, know, at least experientially, what the term resistance means. Resistance means that a person, in a therapeutic process, no longer feels like growing. Walls are built around sensitive areas, sacred cows, prized values, comfortable old ways of doing things. Resistance is "our child" getting the better of us, to use a term from Eric Berne's *Transactional Analysis*. The child says *no* to the future, *no* to new ways, *no* to health, *no* to relief from painful ways of living, often *no* to God. Resistance happens to any of us serious about our own growth. Freud spoke of "the beloved symptoms," as a way of expressing that we prefer to hold onto old painful ways of living rather than to risk trying new ways.

On the wall of Gateway House, a drug rehabilitation center in Chicago, hangs a plaque that reads "I don't care how you feel, act as if . . . . " I have remembered those words for years, because when I saw them they articulated an insight I had stumbled onto experientially. In my own attempts at emotional growth, especially during periods of acute anxiety, I have felt my emotions leading me backward into old ways of feeling and acting. I discovered that for my personality, I had to declare "as if" days. Though, indeed, I might be going through periods of doubt or fear, I could not give in to those feelings. I had to push myself outward, acting *as if*—as if I felt courageous; as if I loved and esteemed myself; as if God loved me. Often I can name the counter attitude and behavior to my fear, doubt, stress or sadness. While I need to name, accept, and integrate whatever emotion is going on within me, that does not mean I need to act on all of them, or be directed by them. I have found that the opposite is true, I need to act on the "counter feeling" of the painful emotion. If filled with doubt, I need to act as if I am convinced. If self-doubting, I need to act as if I am courageous. If feeling unloved, I need to act as if I am lovable. If I feel God does not love me, I need to act as if he does. If feeling anxious, I need to act as if I am peaceful. If feeling depressed, I need to act as if I am joyful.

I am not advocating a new form of neurosis or psychosis, but rather a variation on the theme of behavior modification. The therapists at Gateway House, trying to lead adolescents and young adults from drug addiction to freedom, know that if left to their feelings, their clients would immediately begin smoking marijuana, snorting cocaine, or shooting heroin. They need to help their clients name and identify the feelings that lead to substance abuse, then to glimpse the counter feelings that are healthy and addiction-free. Then those counter feelings need to be gradually approached, gradually assimilated by acting "as if." Acting as if has a way of melting or gradually eroding problematic networks of emotions, and gradually turning one's interior world around. Acting as if, is, in essence, living out the ideal with the hope that our heads and hearts will catch up with our behavior. It is behavior leading the charge of growth, with emotions and convictions following. It is pre-planned behavior change that flows from listening and insight. Finally, "acting as if" leads us back to Bernard Tyrrell's principle from *Christology II*. If a person really wants to grow, he or she needs to develop the will to discomfort, much like an athlete or body builder whose will to discomfort can empower him or her to forgo momentary, immediate gratification with an eye set on the greater reward that awaits one on the other side of a period of self-discipline.

Scriptural Images of Behavior Change

The image of letting go of something, leaving something, is very strong in the scriptural accounts of growth, conversion, and transformation. Abraham is called to leave his homeland, at an old age, to form a nation. Moses is called to let go of anonymity and security to lead his people out of bondage. Jeremiah and the other prophets heard deep calls within themselves to leave the status quo of their lives for a new and challenging future. Jesus experienced the ultimate letting go of security in moving toward Jerusalem that first Palm Sunday, then in shedding ego and physical life on the cross. Paul had his plans and life itinerary re-routed as he journeyed toward Damascus. In each case, there was the need to not only change head and heart, but also behavior. With the integration of interior change and behavior change, the Spirit of God was allowed to work in transforming ways to create, to bring new life to the individual and those connected with him.

I intend to spend more time and space on this later, but I will, nonetheless, mention it here also. Prayer is an environment, a milieu, an experience, a context in which I can find energy and power for behavior change. Prayer can become time and space for me to listen, gain insight, make decisions, and covenant for behavior change. More specifically, prayer can be a time to gain energy for "acting as if." The psycho-therapist Adeline Starr, whose expertise is in group therapy, speaks of a group process called psycho-drama as an opportunity for hurting people to rehearse for life together. I think Starr's phrase "rehearsal for life" applies also to prayer. In prayer that is oriented toward genuine conversion and spiritual transformation, I invite the healing power of God into wounded emotions to help me achieve what I cannot achieve by myself.

Conclusion

Whenever I speak of the need to join changed hearts and minds to changed behavior, and to do all of that in the context of prayer, I am reminded of Paul's phrase "to put on the Lord Jesus." Paul is speaking of Jesus as a *persona* to be put over all the other overlays and aspects of personality—almost to be worn like a new coat. Paul's reference to "putting on" reminds us of something that we have spoken of throughout this chapter. Living with new attitudes, values, and lifestyles necessitates our *putting on* at times, living in such a way that is foreign to our con-ditioning, to our rote ways of doing life. So much of emotional-spiritual growth involves our casting off of "childish" ways to "put on" the full, mature humanity of Jesus.

Anyone with even a glimmer of scriptural knowl-edge, knows that what we have spoken of in this chapter—changed hearts and changed behavior—is a mirroring of the message of the prophets, the great penitential psalms, and the preaching of Jesus. I have been speaking essentially of repentance, turning away from often subtle sin, and turning toward the values and Spirit of Jesus. To speak of repentance on the level of our emotional selves might seem incongruous to people more accustomed to thinking that religion and life are separate realities. The unfolding vision of this study is more in line with the theological views of Karl Rahner and Gregory Baum and others who tried to topple the spiritual two-story universe many of us were raised in—with life serving as the first floor, and religion as the second floor. The issues which are most religious and most spiritual are those at the heart of what it means to be human—questions like Who am I? What is the meaning of life? Why do we suffer and die? Is there a more peaceful and truthful way for me to live than the way I am living now? Conversion happens through the most human feelings, thoughts, and experiences of our lives. It is to *conversion* that we more fully direct our attention.

CHAPTER THREE
Seasons of Conversion

REMEMBER the days when we thought conversion was changing denominations? More than Catholics becoming Protestant or Jewish, or vice versa, conversion is the very essence of any emotional or spiritual growth. To talk about conversion we need to create briefly some theological and psychological undergirding. Let us turn to some contemporary writers.

Gregory Baum, referred to in a previous chapter, in his book *Man Becoming*, spoke of the Jesus perspective, or insight, into the nature of God. God is not "totally out there." Our God is a God of immanence, present and alive in human experience. John Shea has certainly re-echoed that vision in his books *Stories of God, Stories of Faith*, and *An Experience Called Spirit*. Shea encourages us to be sensitive to our most human moments as opportunities to experience this immanent God. Paul Tillich provided an important insight in one of his volumes of *Systematic Theology* when he spoke of the ministry of evangelization as helping people with the conversion process. Tillich explained the conversion process as a "waking up experience." Conversion is waking up to "the Spiritual Presence"—that immanent God, with us in our human experience and moments. Emilie Griffin's book, *Turning: Reflections on Conversion*, offers helpful terms for articulating what conversion looks and feels like. She says that most conversion experiences involve: 1) an inner experience of "ache" or wanting something more out of life; 2) a period of spiritual, religious investigation; 3) some experience of struggle, or the "collapse" of one's world; 4) a surrender to a new experience and understanding of God.

A priest from the Archdiocese of Chicago, Fr. Edward Braxton, wrote a popular and insightful book on growth in faith entitled *The Wisdom Community*. In the book, Braxton looks at the experience of conversion, building on some of the insights of Bernard Lonergan. He speaks of patterns, or the many thresholds for conversion, present in people's human moments. For some, their *physical condition* is a springboard for conversion; others experience a *psychological pattern*—that is, their feelings lead them to deeper immersion into life's mysteries. Others have a more directly *mystical experience*; while others report *relationships* or *intellectual searching* serving as springboards to conversion. When we find ourselves in these or other human patterns that Braxton mentions, we can respond with *agnosticism* (indifference about God), atheism (denial of the reality of God), *idolatry* (giving others or things the attention due God alone), or *conversion*.

Braxton suggests that people in the midst of conversion sense mystery present at the core of their experience. They gradually begin to name the mystery *God*. The process can progress to an awareness that Jesus is the fullest revelation of this God. Such encounters with God challenge us to change our ways of feeling, thinking, and valuing. Such interior change can lead also to a change of behavior and lifestyle. *The phenomenon that facilitates a conversion response to human experience is the presence of a wisdom community, or people of faith, with whom we can dialogue and pray about our life experiences.*

Finally, James Fowler, whose work has significantly influenced religious education in recent years, offers interesting insights into the conversion process. *He says that in conversion there is 1) a revolution of one's value system; 2) a revolution of what one perceives as power; and 3) a revolution of the master stories and images by which we interpret our lives.*

With the previous survey of ideas as a foundation I would like to offer four areas of our lives that are crucial for us who are interested in developing a spirituality for an anxious age. These four areas are: 1) *the natural invitations to conversion that arise out of the aging process, or the developmental life cycle that all of us are involved in; 2) the opportunities for conversion arising out of major or minor life accidents; 3) the experience of "catching one's self" in a process of deterioration or disintegration on some level of life, and doing something to turn one's life around (this is the experience of repentance); 4) the very human experience of longing, often for something vague, that is indeed a disguised longing for God.*

Natural Invitations to Conversion Through the Developmental Stages of the Life Cycle

Patti, several years ago, told me that she did not understand herself very well anymore. She was nearing forty, and suddenly felt a spurt of independence that she has never experienced before. In friendships, marriage, parenting, and also in work, she no longer felt like "someone's daughter, someone's wife, someone's something." She felt, for the first time in her life, that she was her own person—with her own identity, values, needs, and wants. She also reported feeling differently about God and Church. She felt that in the past her spirituality was largely rooted in feelings of guilt and obligation. She noticed a transformation taking place. She was moving from the "gotta" stage to the "wanta" stage. She went to Church, because she felt that she needed and wanted the experience. Amid all this internal confusion, she articulated a very real question: "What is happening to me?"

I think what was happening to her is what happens to a lot of women in their late thirties: she was beginning to break out of the "Cinderella Complex" and emerge into her own unique identity. And that experience of *women*, which seems typical of those previous generations of women whose early adulthood was largely culturally stereotyped, is similar to an experience rather common to all of us at many different times in our life cycle. In short, we age. As we age, we change internally. As we change internally, in values and feelings, our concept and experience of God often change. Developmental changes seem to be natural invitation times to experience conversion. The "felt experience" of the conversion process is that of "an awakening," or waking up to something not recognized before.

Roger Gould, in his book *Transformations*, speaks

of the evolution or change of vision that frequently accompanies growth and aging. The changing vision that he describes is largely an *emotional response to one's world.* He says we carry within us emotionally tinged assumptions that the relentless aging process constantly challenges. The period from age 16 to 22 is a confrontation of the assumption "We'll always live with our parents and be their child." This stage involves the beginning of leaving the parental, familial world. The period of 22 to 28 confronts the assumption "My parents will always be there to help me if I can't do it on my own." The *"Opening Up to What's Inside Stage"* (28-34), confronts the assumption "My parents simplified view of my inner reality is the correct one." The flip side of that is experienced during the late twenties and early thirties, when we begin to deal with *the complexities of our emotional makeup and personalities.* The stage of *mid-life,* with its felt limitations and turmoil, brings us head-on with the assumption: "There is not any real death or evil in the world." Our parents' deaths, and the death of other friends and family members, bouts with limits and sickness within ourselves, unmask the lack of truth in such an attempt at denying the reality of one's self.

Gail Sheehy's book, *Pathfinders,* uses other words to describe what it feels like to "go through a stage of transition." She speaks of four typical steps one moves through in the process. They are:

1) *anticipation:* an interior, felt experience
   that aging is bringing with it some obvious

changes in the self concept, self ideal,
and mode of living;

2) *separation:* an actual leaving of old ways
of being and doing, so that one might
explore new possibilities and opportunities
for the self;

3) *incubation:* this is an experimentation
phase in which the person in a life stage
transition tries on new attitudes and behavioral patterns;

4) *incorporation:* after an appropriate period of
time, unique to each individual, the person
begins to solidify those parts of the new self
that seem the most effective and functional
in reality.

What is the relevance of all this "life change talk"
to our topic of conversion? I believe the upheavals
that we experience in passing from one stage to
another—upheavals that may be great in some and
not as greatly felt in others—are *Kairos* moments in
which we can confront a tension in most of our lives.
The tension is between the *false self* and the *true self,*
illusion and *truth,* the *ladder of success* and *achievement* and the *spiral of deepening spirituality, faulty
vision* and *Kingdom/Good News vision* for life.

There is an often painful process of individuation
going on in most of our lives. A life transition, rather
than a phenomenon of the pop psychological culture,
is a critical experience for us as individuals and the

relational and/or family systems we are part of. The values and insights of Jesus and the Judaeo-Christian tradition offer meaning for our often lonely life journey. We especially need to see in our crises the *opportunities* present in the struggle, especially the *opportunities for conversion.*

The life stage transitions always include a tension. The tension is between what I previously referred to as "the false self" and the "true self." The false self is made up of the internal rules and external roles that life teaches us to base our lives on. The false self is a depository from the culture and society of "shoulds," "oughts," "have tos," and "musts." The false self is the internal "tyrant" or "dictator" that controls our thoughts, feelings, and actions. It is the false self that triggers pain, frustrations, anger, and disappointment in us.

The "true self" is the self conformed to the image of Jesus Christ. It is a self that lives with his vision of the Father's love, the pervasiveness of the Spirit, the universal community of persons, the imperative of a just society, and the hope of the life that only comes through death. *The true self is only gradually and partially achieved by: a) risking to internalize his vision in preference to our own "false vision of self"; and b) practicing that vision in behavior and lifestyle.*

The false-self true-self tension is the tension between the God of light and manna and the golden calf of the People of God in the desert. The felt and perceived upheaval of a life transition can be a time of conversion, conversion from the false self to the self shedding its illusions.

Life Accidents as Invitations to Conversion

In *Pathfinders*, Sheehy talks about *life accidents*—those events in life that we do not plan or bargain for. Life accidents are the experiences of pain, disappointment, frustration, or loss that enter life without our inviting them. The *Book of Job* is a story of life accidents. Job is visited by a series of crises and catastrophes. He and his friends spend much of the *Book of Job* wondering *why*—why does God allow tragedy to enter the lives of good people. A young man, Elihu, enters toward the end of the book and critiques the "why-wondering" of the men, challenging them to realize that the plan of God and the mystery of life can never be completely understood. Job speaks a key insight toward the end of the book. He says that before his suffering he only knew God by hearsay, but through his struggle he came to know God face to face.

Life accidents contain within themselves the potential of moving a person from the God of hearsay to the God of personal experience. Ministry to "life accident" moments, while admitting time for emotional breathing and ventilation on the part of those involved in the accident, does have a unique orientation. *The orientation is toward uncovering the God of life present in death moments.* In life accident moments we all have the tendency to do what Jesus did on the cross—bounce between feelings of abandonment and faith-filled surrender. Put another way: in life accidents, there is always a tension between a destructive response and a positive one. A gospel response to a life accident senses the unconditional love of the Father, the paschal mystery of Jesus, and the creative force of the Spirit present in moments of brokenness.

The role of ministry is to help believers make sense of their lives when they are in crisis. Ministry in the Church tries to help facilitate a creative response to the unexpected and disappointing. Conversion-centered ministry helps people to have the Job-experience: the movement through a life accident from a God of hearsay to a God of personal experience.

Patti a Few Years Later: Another Conversion

Patti again serves as a model for this discussion of the conversion process. While she was in the midst of moving toward resolution of her life-stage-induced conversion—a conversion especially to the want-to God, instead of the gotta God, Patti experienced a life accident. Steve, her teen-age son, always a hulk of a young man, began to experience annoying health problems—a flu that would not relent. One doctor's diagnosis labeled the lingering malaise of body and spirit as a persistent infection. Another speculated about hepatitis. Steve's weight loss and inability to function normally led the family to seek additional professional advice. Hospitalization, more testing, and a greater degree of honesty from the young man about the extent of his symptoms revealed more alarming news. Steve had a rare form of cancer anchored in his glandular system, and spreading rapidly.

Within a month, Patti's eldest child, of three, was

dead. Cancer ravaged him like a demon, like a brush
fire. She who was just completing a kind of resolution of one phase of her conversion journey, began
another leg of the journey, almost without time for a
breath. Patti, and Ernie, her husband, stood by their
son daily—trying their best, yet realizing there was
nothing they could do. If Patti's previous leg of the
conversion journey was a journey toward a deeper
experience and shaping of self-hood, the death of her
son was a more passionate and faith-filled immersion in mystery. The God who gave her courage to
stand by her disintegrating son remained and remains a mystery to her. Yet he was her source of
courage and strength through her son's struggles,
and the love source she finally wanted to surrender
Steve to.

When I see Patti and Ernie now, months after
Steve's death, there is still pain in their eyes. As Patti
said recently, the pain of the loss of a child does not
get easier. Rather, it gets more painful as the reality
and finality of the death settles in. Her experience
of God now is one much more congruent with Braxton's idea of the Wisdom Community—though her
beautifully simple south-side Chicago faith would
never permit her to use some of his on-target, but
complex, religious language. In a not yet articulated
way, she knows that God was the source of energy
that got her through the ordeal of Steve's final days
and the funeral. But she also knows that the God of
love appeared for her and her family in the form of
caring relationships, specifically family members,
neighbors, and fellow parishioners who stood by the

family and continue to do so, helping them to make sense out of nonsense.

Patti and Ernie's experience is what Braxton calls *ecclesial conversion*, or the experience that the Jesus, who helps me to name my numinous experiences "God," is someone incarnated and alive in faith-filled relationships in the Christian community.

The Life Accident and Anxiety

Perhaps no conversion threshold is more relevant for the person prone to anxiety difficulties than the *life accident*. I did a radio program recently on what I called "what if-ism." I based the program on some of my own neurotic struggles. Sometimes triggered by overwork, sometimes by fatigue, I can go through rather painful experiences or seasons of "the what ifs." The "what ifs" is a term I use to describe those periods some of us go through in which we expect —indeed fear the worst—from life. Life's negative possibilities lurk as ghosts—sometimes very specific in our consciousness, other times appearing as free-floating anxiety.

Phobics, or those prone to anxiety attacks, are especially sensitized to the possibilities of a life acci-dent. Behind every life accident story is the ex-perience of some loss—the loss of a loved one, prestige, the status quo of one's life, something or someone that has become beloved. Current research suggests that phobics, somewhere in their past, have experienced a significant loss, or intuitively feel the impending pain of loss and try to control such situations to avoid that pain. Phobics, indeed many experiencing anxiety or stress, often those suffering from depression, many in emotional turmoil, are dealing with a "loss consciousness." So many in contemporary society are anxiously trying to avoid perceived catastrophes, or trying to recover from perceived loss.

No matter how much or how often we try to control life, we discover that we cannot. The essence of the mystery of life is that it is filled with life accidents over which we do not have a lot of control. In developing a genuinely Christian approach to the age of anxiety, believers come to see the life accident in a radically new and different way. Life accidents come to be seen first of all as inevitable. Trying to resist or sidestep them generates only negative, destructive energy. Secondly, life accidents come to be seen as opportunities—opportunities to learn, grow, and experience the God of life calling us in new, challenging directions.

Barbie: Discovering a New Experience of God in the Life Accident

I received a call recently from one of Chicago's largest hospitals. I was immediately on alert when I saw the message, because the hospital was not one of my parish's local centers for healing, but rather one of the area's major research hospitals. The note urgently asked me to call Barbie's mother. Barbie is one of our parish's twelve-year-old girls. When I arrived at the hospital, Bob and Betty, Barbie's parents, told me about their dilemma. Little over a week before, the little girl had begun to experience a tingling, then vague aches in her legs. Just a few days later, she began to fall involuntarily when she walked—unable to control her own movement. Medical investigations revealed a growth within her spinal column. That wintry day, Bob and Betty spoke of their hope that God would allow the tumor to be benign. But they revealed also a faith-filled openness that they could continue to trust God even if the tests revealed malignancy.

Their faith was soon put to the test. Within five days, the tests came back revealing an apparently contained but nonetheless threatening malignancy in the little girl's spinal column. When I stopped over with communion for Barbie, a few days after the bad news arrived, Barbie revealed an adolescent self-consciousness thrust into the depths of life's mysteries. She wondered aloud about her social status, when chemotherapy would rob her of her hair. But then she spoke of hope, and her conviction that God was on her side, and would help her even through the worst of times.

Barbie's parents communicated similar sentiments. Bob spoke of a specifically delineated time, fifteen minutes, when, after the diagnosis of the malignancy, he was angry at God. Then, he says, the cloud of resentment lifted; and he began to see God in a different light. Rather than the grand puppeteer causing Barbie's problems, God became for Bob, the healing force, much akin to the God source spoken of in Harold Kushner's *When Bad Things Happen to Good People.* In Kushner's view, bad things simply happen in the course of good people's lives. Rather than the source of those problems, God is a source of encouragement when those bad times indeed do happen.

The life accident can be a crucible in which the heart is purified, the life vision clarified, and the personal vision of God altered—more in conformity with Jesus' vision of God.

Catching One's Self: Another Threshold

So many scenes from the classic movie *Gone With the Wind* have stayed with me. One in particular involved Scarlett O'Hara groveling in the dirt for a potato to eat after the war had destroyed her family and wealth. As the camera moves away from her, she lifts her fist to the sky, and with passionate anger proclaims to life that she will not continue to live in this fashion.

The persona of Scarlett is not a model that I am suggesting for healthy living. But that one scene in which she angrily re-directs her life deserves some comment. Anger, channeled properly, can be a creative emotion. As with any emotion, anger is an energy, an energy that can be put to destructive or creative use. I frequently counsel people to make a decision and then follow through in behavior to transform emotional energies like worry, stress, or sadness into a healthy anger that begins to move them in a more positive direction.

Anger is not the only avenue to go down in experiencing the threshold of conversion I am speaking of here. It is one of many avenues. I borrow a term from Alfred Adler, Rudolf Dreikurs, and the Adlerian school of psychotherapy in saying: conversion happens when anger or some other rational or emotive energy helps us to "catch ourselves" in a pattern of non-growth or deterioration and re-direct ourselves toward new life.

One of my least favorite experiences in life is going to the dentist. Recently, I had to go through long-term dental care because my aversion to the dentist led me to procrastinate about seeing him for years. Unconsciously, I "let part of myself go"; with the consequence of that part of my life literally deteriorating. What I allowed to happen to my wisdom tooth happens to many different parts of our lives. We let our marriages go, our friendships go, our health go, our moral integrity go. We fail to attend to the quality of certain parts of our lives. We allow unchecked habits or a conditioned self to rob the best self of life and spirit.

I spoke earlier of William James's two notions of conversion: conversions of surrender and volitional conversion. Conversions of surrender are similar to what we have discussed already under the themes of "life stage transition conversions" and "life accident conversions." In such conversions of surrender, we are more or less robbed of control, or at least perceive ourselves as not totally in control. We begin to sense a "more than ourselves" mystery, which the Christian story and tradition has taught us to name God, Abba, Father. Volitional conversions, or "catching yourself" conversions, are rather experiences of retrieving control over our lives, a control perhaps that we have relinquished to some demonic or limiting force in our lives. "Catching yourself conversions" involve a naming of the growth-blocking forces in our lives, a decision to do something about the situation, new behaviors that flow from the decision and attitude change, and the conscious harnessing of emotional energies in a new direction. Volitional conversions also include in part a practicing of a stance of surrender, or reliance on the Spirit of God for healing those parts of ourselves we have trouble getting at ourselves. This type of conversion experience is perhaps best understood by referring to the prophetic notion of repentance. The Jewish nation was consistently reminded by the prophets, including Jesus, that what God wanted of them was not empty ritual, but rather a radical change of mind, heart, and behavior.

Gerald May, in his book, *Will and Spirit*, captures well the relationship between the types of conversion that we have been discussing in two pregnant words, *willfulness* and *willingness*. May's notion of *willfulness* refers to the capacity we indeed do have to change our lives by decision, attitude and behavior change, and the harnessing of emotional energies. Willfulness refers to what we can do. Willingness, on the other hand, refers to the experience we all have of our own limits, what we can and *cannot* do, and our need to "let go" into the "more than ourselves" that we believe and hope to be ultimate love.

Longing: Another Threshold

For several years I have frequently found myself longing for something, someone. Parish life became too restricting, so I accepted offers to minister on the diocesan level. Diocesan ministry became too sterile, so I accepted offers to teach at several graduate schools. Longing for the presence of children and heterogeneous relationships led me back to part-time parish duties. My odyssey has convinced me of something: the human heart is indeed hungry and thirsty. That is why Jesus frequently encased his revelation of God and the Kingdom in terms of food and drink. He knew most of us are looking for something, for someone. My insatiable hunger and thirst for multiple experiences has convinced me I am actually longing for the someone who is present within, beyond, and behind all those experiences: the God of Jesus.

St. Augustine spoke of the *longing phenomenon* in his *Confessions*. He speaks of having sought God all through his lifetime. But the search often took him down side roads, or to what amounted to masks or disguises of God. After his initial conversion, he spoke of finally having tasted the God he long sought. After experiencing the true God, he longed for more. A similar journey of faith is documented in Monika Furlong's *Merton: A Biography*. Thomas Merton, the paradigmatic young agnostic, is followed through his longings and turns in the road to a lifestyle of radical, ongoing conversion. What Furlong portrays in her biographical analysis is a man "obsessed with God," unconsciously *obsessed*, or *longing* for most of his life.

The Process of Spirituality

What I hope is evident from the discussion of the four conversion thresholds is that in most of us conversion is "in process." In the notion of process, Catholic praxis and theology diverts from popular fundamentalist notions of conversion. It seems that fundamentalism stresses "arrival," or a steady diet of a "willful" mind-set. In their orientation, the emphasis is on the particular time a person decides for God. In a Catholic, or alternate context, such willful moments would have to become part of a larger fabric that includes life transitions, life accidents, and times when, at least appparently, God is choosing what to do with us.

Building on previous references to Adler's notion of the lifestyle, let me venture a definition of *spirituality*. Spirituality refers to the core of a person that makes him or her tick, the value system, the behavior pattern that flows from the value system. It is impossible for someone to not be spiritual in this context. We all have a core, a motivating center, a code of inner rules, a cast of roles that we play. We are all hungry and thirsty, quite often like Augustine and Merton, trying to satisfy these deepest of hungers and thirsts with that which can only partially satisfy.

One's spirituality is indeed in process, evolving. Admittedly we all pass through periods when it seems our *rules* and *roles* are apparently cast in stone. But for most of us the lifestyle or spirituality is porous and incomplete—capable of penetration and adaptation. If I could venture an indictment against American organized religions, it would be that we are a nation of agnostics and idolators. We profess the centuries-old creeds and symbolic systems of our traditions, but our behavior patterns indicate that even the so-called Christians among us are motivated by forces other than Jesus. We attempt to live the Jesus vision without conversion. We try to be spiritual without conforming our *rules* and *roles* to the values and vision of the *Kingdom*. Whether it be through the aging process, surprises in life, life decisions, or tapping into our deepest human longings, we are constantly invited to move from our agnostic or idolatrous spiritualities to the spirituality of the Kingdom.

Conversion Toward Social Justice

If there has been any obvious weakness in our Catholic approach to conversion spirituality, it has been a pre-occupation with the *self*. Certainly the focus of attention and change in a conversion process is the self. But we need to be cautious that we do not see as the goal of all conversion processes perfect self-fulfillment and self-actualization. Such an approach to spirituality is a mirroring of the forces of narcissism so prevalent in American culture.

The theologian Bernard Lonergan speaks of conversion in three different categories: intellectual conversion, religious conversion, and moral conversion. Intellectual conversion is a turning more toward the truth about life. Religious conversion is a turning, in love, more fully toward the God of mystery. Moral conversion speaks of a change in behavior. Specifically, the words that I mouth, flowing from intellectual and religious conversion, I begin to live out in my daily actions. Moral conversion involves a concern for "a more than ourselves," for the world and people around us—near and far.

Conversion in its most highly developed phase is a movement into a new consciousness—a global consciousness. In that consciousness there is a concern for the quality of life, the course of our world, and especially for the poor and needy throughout our world. Conversion is incomplete without a concern for the transformation, not only of ourselves as individuals, but also the transformation of our world. The needs of the world become items for our prayer, our compassion, and our service.

A topic that I will refer to later is the need for the anxious, stressful, or depressed person to "get off the self," or "transcend the self" to experience genuine concern and love for others. Part of the anxious-depressed syndrome is a "closing in on the self," a pre-occupation with the self. Concern for service or social justice can be a sign or symptom that someone is converting from inner logic that contributes to emotional pain and narcissism. But such concern can also be part of the very therapy that relieves the emotional pain.

Conclusion: Risky Business

The play and movie, *Mass Appeal*, features two characters, Monsignor Farley, an aging, alcoholic pastor and Mark, a rebellious, searching seminarian. Mark is sent by the seminary to Farley's parish to be "straightened out" by the old man. They have many conflicts throughout the story because of their divergent views on most issues. But as the story unfolds, it is obvious that the old priest is also attracted to the searching faith of the young man.

One night, through alcohol-induced tears, Farley reveals his inner world. Referring to his own preaching, Farley says: "You know, when I was your age, I had something to say, but I didn't know how to say it Now, I know how to say it, but I don't have anything to say." The scene has stayed with me, because I thought it was a touching portrayal of a person trapped in interior stagnation, a person who has given up on emotional and spiritual risks. The resolution of the dramatic conflict is that Farley, at the end of the play, becomes a person who is willing to risk again.

I was struck by the news coverage in early 1984 of the great risks the people of Poland endured in the name of publicly displaying the cross. The Communist leaders, with threats, coercion, and incarceration tried to stifle the Poles' centuries-old faith. Their risking in the name of the cross reminded me of the feeling tone of the first cross, raised on a Jerusalem hill the first Good Friday. Jesus risked, and his cross endures as a symbol and reminder of his risking. The final journey toward Jerusalem was a risk, but he apparently felt he had to do it—to be true to his own inner world and to fulfill the Father's will for him.

Any spirituality that pretends to be Christian must be cross spirituality, that is risky spirituality. Conversion demands that we need to die to something, let go of something, get rid of something, transform something, if we are to "rise" to newness of life. While much of this chapter might sound like conversion is easy, the truth is that no schema about conversion can accurately represent the pain, anger, or risk involved in being willing to "die" that new life might happen. Conversion spirituality is indeed paschal, that is, passage in nature. It is always a movement through death, however it appears in a given life situation, on to new life. The most evocative symbol of conversion is the cross. It reminds us of the risky nature of true conversion. It challenges us to not protect ourselves from growth with our own self-created safe crosses.

We need at this point a clearer picture of what it is that we of the nervous, worried, uptight, sad age can convert to. What is worth risking for? What does a healthier, more positive approach to life look like? We turn to that now as we try to discern just what it was that "made Jesus tick."

CHAPTER FOUR
Visions and the Vision

I WRITE about anxiety in this book from a wealth of experience. The experience has not just included my attempts to help anxious others. Rather, much of my insight flows from having wrestled with the symptoms and motivating conflicts of anxiety for years in my own life. The first obvious onset of symptoms for me occurred in my early twenties. I had known for years what it felt like to be afraid, lonely, or anxious about something. But fear, in previous years, had usually had a focus or target. As I moved into young adulthood, I began to have such feelings, unattached to obvious stimuli. The anxiety was of a free-floating nature. It felt something like: "There is something bothering me, but I don't know exactly what it is." Those vague waves or clouds of anxiety gave way to very acute feelings of panic with accompanying physical symptoms. The physical symptoms were quite frightening: nausea, dizziness, sweating, heart palpitations.

Physical symptoms and accompanying anxiety can become so powerful that they develop an autonomy all their own. Sufferers can develop a secondary kind of fear that amounts to being afraid of being afraid. Then, to avoid the symptoms, people tend to develop strategies of avoiding the situations that seem to provoke the frightening experience of an anxiety attack. When the condition has progressed this far, frequently sufferers start to excuse themselves from social situations, avoid some relationships and prefer to be placed, physically or geographically, in a situation that is perceived as secure. When one has gotten into the secondary fear pattern of trying to avoid symptoms, that is, the fear of being afraid, a form of paralysis has already set in. No longer is such a person living life freely and fully. Rather, his or her primary goal has become "how to avoid certain people, places or things—how to avoid being afraid."

My own situation led me to sleep a lot. One day, when I was twenty-three, a school counselor at the graduate school where I was studying, came to my room. He had become a friend, and was aware of my current phobias and problems. He found me in bed in mid-day, and inquired *why*. I told him I was particularly nervous that day, and had gone to bed to escape. He challenged me. I could no longer escape my situation. I had to enter into it, understand it, and do something about it. I got out of bed and called the president of the theological school to request funding and support for counseling. I had a problem, and I was going to do something about it. I had no idea of the depth and length of the journey that I began that day. The school official consented to see me on my birthday. We agreed upon a counselor I would consult. My birthday that year was the beginning of an agonizing gestation, but a genuine re-birth.

Physical Symptoms: Penetrating the Facade

My first intuition, upon beginning a therapeutic relationship, was that it would be quick and easy.

There was some simple thing causing anxiety within me. The therapist would be able to help me deal with it rather easily. I even hoped that through hypnosis, I might be able to almost magically "turn the anxiety off" through my own volition. I did not understand the intricate networking of psychological factors that made me an anxious person. I did not realize something which Claire Weekes has written about extensively in her books on anxiety: that indeed some people are physiologically predisposed to greater experiences of anxiety or stress. Recent research into biochemical imbalances have re-inforced Weekes' insight that physiology can be at the root of some anxiety and stress. Recent research has shown this is true not only in the case of anxiety and stress, but also depression.

In short, physical symptoms can result from attitudes, convictions or values that are anxiety oriented, or one's physical make-up can be extremely sensitized and prone to anxiety symptoms. Physical symptoms can in turn be the source of greater anxiety. The point in considering this emotional-physical tension is to at least partially portray the vicious circle in which those in emotional pain can find themselves. Internal chaos contributes to physical discomfort; physical discomfort can in turn induce, re-inforce, or exacerbate internal emotional chaos. And physical symptoms can become free-standing sources of pain and avoidance strategies.

I entered a therapeutic relationship with the agenda of getting rid of my pain, especially my physical symptoms. The therapist was and is a wise yet confrontative man who was quite aware of the syndrome or pattern that was inhibiting me. He did not want to spend a great deal of time talking about symptoms. He doubted neither their reality nor the pain connected with them. But he knew that behind the symptoms were a lot of intangible ideas, feelings, and convictions that were at the core of the anxiety pattern. So, while trying to patiently listen to the stories of panic attacks, he would sometimes gently, sometimes aggressively try to push me beyond the attacks to look and listen beyond the obvious to the hidden, the subtle, the repressed.

I thought of my earlier self in a recent group therapy session that I was conducting. We were considering the initial point of this book—the importance of learning to listen to one's self. One of the women in the group honestly confessed: "I would rather do anything than to make the time and effort to listen to myself." Why is that? Why is it that so many of us find listening to self so difficult? Why is it that someone with anxiety symptoms would rather focus on the symptoms than look at the possible cause of the symptoms? There are several possible answers to these questions.

The dimensions of the preconscious, subconscious, and unconscious are still experienced as a giant abyss or chasm within us. So often the abyss looms before us, and the bottom of the pit is not even within sight. The abyss is dark and frightening. It is the receptacle of many years of hurt, fears, disappointments, sins, and guilt. In other words, you do not exactly know who or what you will bump into when you venture deeply into the self. The image of Scripture that I am reminded of relative to the inner abyss is the desert. As Jesus did when he entered the desert, so also we in entering ourselves meet both the divine and the demonic. The desert can be a frightening place to enter alone—until you get used to it.

Freud had another insight into pre-occupation with symptoms when he spoke of "the beloved symptoms." In this view, a person has a love for the very anxious or depressive condition that he or she complains about. The condition, depsite its pain, has some pay-off, like extra attention, an excuse for over-dependency, or some other form of narcissistic gratification. It is similar to the school-age child who begins to grow comfortable with the cold or the flu because the bout with illness provides an escape from reality.

Alfred Adler offered a development of this theory. Adler believed life consisted of a series of tasks—tasks to be resolved positively. The person in emotional conflict and turmoil is the person having difficulty with the life tasks. The tasks, according to Adler are: feeling good about the self, finding meaningful work, developing a network of friends, developing the capacity for a healthy experience of sexuality and intimacy, and the cosmological task. Adler added the cosmological task rather late in the development of his theory. The cosmological task refers to a person's pursuit of meaning and purpose—in short the quest for a spirituality. Adler felt all of the tasks needed a kind of picture frame—the over-riding task of pursuing the God question.

Adler saw pre-occupation with symptoms as an attempt to sidestep one or more of the tasks. So, for Adler, symptom pre-occupation was the smoke that led directly back to the fire of difficulties with the self, work, friendship, love, or life's meaning.

In short, anxiety and stress, and depression as well, often come attached to physical difficulties. While physical problems sometime lie at the very root of the emotional disorder, sometimes also they are symptomatic of deeper, hidden problems. For many people healing only lies in entering the abyss, the desert within. This becomes even more difficult when symptoms become almost a free-standing disorder on their own. To penetrate the facade of symptoms, to look and listen more deeply is quite difficult. It is not impossible, however. It simply requires a great deal of courage.

Discoveries in the Desert

I became quite discouraged when I found out emotional healing was not like freeze dried, instant coffee—something that would happen with the blinking of an eye, or the popping of a pill. It was only slowly that I caught on that my helper did not want to hear about each detail of my anxiety attacks, but wanted rather to talk about what was going on in my life, and what had gone on in my life. And it was much later that I saw the correlation between the pain I articulated in my stories and the pain I was experiencing emotionally and quite often physically. It took me a long time to realize the anxiety attacks, the whole anxiety syndrome, was a mirror image of the life pattern that I had created for myself. It took a long time for me to realize that at the root of my anxieties was a vision problem. My outlook on life was radically in need of re-adjustment.

I had grown up, the second (and last) born of two sons, in a traditional Irish Catholic environment on the southwest side of Chicago. That familial context carried with it all the blessings and curses of other typical Irish Catholic families. I was an asthmatic by age two, a condition apparently genetically transmitted on my father's side of the family. The asthmatic situation seriously limited physical activity, specifically athletic involvement. This was indeed a curse for a young man growing up in the blue collar city of the 50's and 60's. For years, I felt myself in the shadow of my brother, a year-and-a-half my senior. He was a natural athlete; and, though not a disciplined student, was intellectually quicker than I. In hindsight now, I know I had tremendous feelings of competition toward him. I wanted to be like he was. I wanted to be loved and respected by my father, as I perceived Bill to be.

If allergies and wheezing were to limit my getting to first base, I would find another area of achievement. "I'll do well in school," I thought. The pursuit of E's (excellent in the Catholic school system) and A's became my athletic pursuit. As I advanced in grammar school and high school, I became the natural to get elected to school office, the newspaper, helping programs. Priests got to know my name. The choir, altar boys—thoughts of the priesthood: by age fifteen I was smart, respected, and perfect. And I was going to keep it that way, because it brought with it great payoff.

Again in hindsight I can see periods of fear in my childhood and adolescence. In childhood, a terrible summer storm severely damaged our home, while tornadoes took lives in a neighborhood close by. I remember my entire family sleeping with our clothes on, sitting up. I wept that night at the unpredictability of life. I wept with fear. I cried those same tears just some months ago at the death of my infant nephew Justin. Again in childhood, the family physician told us my mother had heart trouble, and we had to monitor our behavior to avoid upsetting her. I made the perceptual jump that my behavior directly controlled her living or dying—a tremendous burden for a little boy. Pre-adolescence and adolescence ushered in huge problems with scrupulosity, multiple confessions, and an obsession with committing mortal sin.

A little boy who needs to get A's, to do and feel the right thing, perceives he has control over and responsibility for the well-being of all, and is under the constantly scrutinizing, judgmental eye of a stern God, grows up to be a man. The vision of self, others, and life, the fearful approach to the life tasks present in me in my early years did not go away. Rather, they grew within me. But as one approaches adulthood, one's childhood perception of things often proves dysfunctional or inadequate for a new stage of development. More specifically, I who thought I could control life and my fears, began in my early twenties to experience life as mysterious, and certainly beyond the rituals of my perfectionism and controlling ways. That disonance between childhood vision of life and budding adult experience of life led me to anxiety attacks that I could use as an excuse to escape from life. It led me ultimately to admit defeat and to seek help in discovering a new vision.

The Lifestyle or Vision of Life

We return to Alfred Adler for a theoretical summary of what I have tried to present through personal example. I was attracted to Adler's personality theory because of its positive view of the human person. Adler was the president of Freud's Psychoanalytic Society in its founding years, but eventually broke from Freud and his circle. For Adler, Freud's theory was too pessimistic. Freud saw the human being as essentially a victim and product of the past and his or her own repressed instinctual drives. Adler's view of person was much more positive.

Adler believed the human person was above all purposive, or directed. In Adlerian thought, the human being is in pursuit of something from the very beginning of life. That something is love and its many variations: belonging, respect, feeling significant. Each of us develops a kind of private logic as to how to feel important and loved. Contained within this private logic, for most of us, are mistaken notions as to what will bring love our way. Many, rather than living out a co-operative "social interest," or people-centered road to love, choose rather a competitive, privatized road, filled with "private logic" life commandments. The paradox in Adlerian therapy is that often what we most earnestly seek, namely loving relationships, remain an elusive goal for many people. And the cause of that is in the mistaken notions of the private logic. Often these involve a compulsion to be better than others, rather than equal to others.

Where do some of the mistaken notions that we operate out of come from? Adlerians emphasize the influence of several factors. The *family constellation* plays a key role. The family constellation refers to the ordinal position one has in the family origin and the psychological repercussions that flow from that position. Rather than the focus on the personal and parenting flaws of mother and father, which Freudians might emphasize, Adlerians focus on the often competitive relationship between siblings. Mother and father are almost like the "carrots" dangled before the children of the family. The parents represent love, affirmation, respect, feelings of significance and importance. Family inter-actions are frequently a kind of "horse race" in pursuit of their esteem.

First-borns tend to be responsible and oriented toward leadership. Second-borns frequently have an Avis-complex, or feel second-best and therefore in need to compete with the first-born, that is, "to try harder." Middle children are "squeezed children," often never feeling the specialness of being oldest or youngest. Youngest children often follow two different patterns. Some become quite dependent and needy, following the "baby script." Others reject that script and become quite independent.

Adlerian theory recognizes differences between the sexes. An only boy in a family of girls tends to be either the "crown prince" or somewhat effeminate.

An only girl in a family of boys tends to be a "little princess" or tomboy. He also postulated that the culturally perceived differences between the sexes resulted in something he called "the masculine protest." The masculine protest has both a male and female expression. Both of these expressions have been vigorously affected by the women's liberation movement. Nonetheless, I believe Adler was correct in his cultural analysis. In the male, the masculine protest expresses itself in a kind of mass-minded, male private logic. It is the experience of struggling to be a real man, with all the machismo connotations connected with it. The female side of the masculine protest is "but I am only a woman," with all the culturally induced inferiority connected with that consciousness. Though both of those mind-sets are vigorously assaulted today, their influence is still felt in human development.

In Adlerian theory, the family constellation, joined to genetic predispositions, early experience, perceptions of the individual, and decisions flowing from those perceptions and experiences, converge to form the lifestyle. The lifestyle is the central theme of Adlerian thought. In a nutshell, the lifestyle is one's vision of life, the rules one plays life by, the roles one plays in life. The lifestyle is lived out with purpose and direction, the achievement of love and significance. As stated earlier, so many people caught in emotionally chaotic and conflictional syndromes reveal a private logic-ridden lifestyle that, in effect, robs them of the very goal they are in pursuit of.

Problematic Lifestyle Types

Certain lifestyle formations lend themselves to anxiety, stress, and depression. If a person wants to know what his or her lifestyle is, a good indication of its orientation can be discerned by completing the following sentences.

"I am . . . . " What does the person think and feel about the self?

"The world, or life is . . . . " What is the individual's outlook on life?

"People are . . . . " What is the generalized approach to people and relationships?

"I must . . . . " What are the moral and ethical convictions of the person?

"I should be . . . . " What are the ideals and strivings of the individual?

The way some people complete these sentences contributes to an unhappy way of life.

"Get an A" people are over-achievers, constantly climbing life's highest peaks, uncomfortable if there are no mountains to climb. Do not take them on vacation.

"Controllers" are obsessive compulsive people, who find their security in their perceived ability to keep other people, life, and God in line. Controllers are like carpet layers. They are constantly trying to "nail life down." Unfortunately when they get one corner down, another corner that they thought was nailed down, curls up on them.

"People pleasers" survive on the crumbs of love
—other peoples' approval. The people pleaser frequently has never had real, substantial experiences
of human love. He or she has grown to mistake the
approval of others for genuine affection. The people
pleaser vacillates between pursuit of approval, anxiety, anger, and depression. All of these emotional
states flow from the impossible task he has set: pleasing everyone.

"Superior people" need to be best at everything.
Their anxiety flows from the possibility of not being
the best. They frequently keep a check on emotional
instability by entering only those fields of experience
wherein they are assured of superiority.

"Heroes, martyrs, and victims" are all variations on
one general personality type: someone with underdeveloped ego strength who finds self-worth in vicar-
iously "living for" a cause or someone else. Heroes
frequently are selflessly obsessed with a cause. Martyrs endure unnecessary pain in the name of some
higher goal. Victims are controlled, indeed pushed
and pulled by their environment, rather than lending
shape and form to it themselves.

"Inferior" people are not objectively lacking in
skills, ability, attractiveness, or any other socially significant attribute. However, they perceive themselves that way. This inferior condition contributes
to feelings of anxiety, stress, or depression.

This list could go on. These six general categories
have been mentioned as a way of making more concrete Adler's notion of the purposeful, directed movement or vision of life called the lifestyle.

Getting in Touch with the Lifestyle

Several counseling sessions can suffice to generate solutions to specific problems. But to begin to re-adjust one's lifestyle requires greater time, effort, and struggle. It frequently requires a therapeutic relationship. The therapist enters a relationship of mutual respect with the client. The therapist needs to be both a source of encouragement and a source of challenge. On the encouragement side, the therapist helps the client to name the personality assets or strengths that he or she has. On the challenge side, therapist and client work on naming, in an equally honest way, the mistaken notions of the private logic that are contributing to emotional and relational disharmony.

Early memories can be retrieved and interpreted —not for their objective truth, but for the subjective perception present in them which in turn contributed to the early formation of the lifestyle. Dreams can be looked at, de-mythologized, and used for helpful insights into a client's preconscious or unconscious world. As the lifestyle begins to stand out in clearer form, client and therapist negotiate on new goals for the client that might contribute toward greater love and peace. Ongoing sessions can provide evaluation of and support for the new journey of growth.

The Lifestyle of Jesus

Jesus lived and died for his lifestyle, such was the

integrity of the man. Unlike most of us, however, Jesus had a name for his lifestyle. He called it the Kingdom of God, or God's reign. We will consider Jesus's experience of the Kingdom under two general categories: Jesus's Perception of Reality and Jesus's Quest.

A) His Perception of Reality

"I have good news for you. The Kingdom of God is at hand. Change your lives, and believe this Good News." These words from the fifteenth verse of Mark's first chapter are an articulation of the heart of Jesus's teaching and ministry. While he begins his ministry in Mark with Kingdom talk, Matthew portrays him as closing his earthly ministry with concern for the Kingdom. Jesus hands over responsibility for the Kingdom to his first disciples, commissioning them to "make disciples" of all the nations. The Kingdom of God is the over-arching symbol of the words and activities of Jesus, summarizing what he was most about. The Kingdom, James Mackey suggests in his book *Jesus: Man & Myth*, is what led to his death. The Kingdom was such a radically different way of looking at reality that it indeed rattled the status quo of both organized religion and government of the day.

Jesus perceived life and reality as shot through with God's Spirit, God's creative influence. That Spirit is for life, for us, not against us. In God is providential care, unconditional love, unrelenting forgiveness. The notion that "God reigns" was Jesus's conviction that we need to build our lives on this love force and on no other foundation. Neither the hopes and illusions of our private logic, nor the false promises of a consumer society, nor some of the institutionalized spiritual distortions of a bureaucratic, institutionalized Church can be foundation for us. They amount, in Jesus' Kingdom vision, to building one's house on sand. In a real sense, one must find the self in and through God. Though the Kingdom obviously has horizontal, community dimensions, a significant part of the Kingdom is vertical and individualized in nature. As Adler saw later in his life, people need to resolve the God question.

If one begins to see life with Kingdom eyes, as Jesus did, then one also begins to experience life as he did. If the reality of *Abba*, Jesus's child-like term for Father, begins to seep into our hearts as well as our heads, we begin to experience life as he did. We begin to "let go" of certain values, convictions, attitudes and the like that restrict us from happiness and tranquility. I take special note when I hear someone describe himself or herself as a survivor. Such a self-concept is incongruent with Kingdom consciousness. Jesus did not say he came to help us survive. Rather he said he came to help us experience "life in the fullest." This is the essence of redemption and salvation. Jesus wants to enter each of our lives and "buy us back" from the forces of sin, illusion, and survival that we might experience fullness of life. Most anxious, stress-filled, depressed people are coping with life, surviving, only partially experiencing life. When one is "born again," as Jesus explains to Nicodemus, one begins to see the Kingdom, *see* God present and active in the human story. Experiencing the God of life propels new Kingdom members to "put away," as Paul says, survival tactics for a more expansive experience of living.

For Kingdom people, "life is dangerous" gives way to "life is joyful." "I have to control" collapses into "I can trust and surrender, because someone out there loves me." "I am unlovable" becomes a changed self-concept: "I know that I am unconditionally accepted and loved." "All people are the same" becomes a new openness to friendship, love, and relationships. "I can't be bothered; I'm too busy" becomes a heartfelt concern for the world around us and the global community. Competition begins to melt into co-operation. Achievement is balanced with an appreciation of the now. Inferiority, superiority, and discrimination are transformed into commitment to the radical equality of all people.

All of the above happens in a process sort of way, through struggle, prayer, and a variety of experiences. The movements described here are not escapes into "situation comedy" type euphoria. They are evolving movements of the human spirit, gradual in nature. Some are a result of the promptings of the Holy Spirit incarnate in human relationships and experiences. Some are of our own choosing as we discover the capacity for self-direction and the many possibilities for us to choose life.

As Jesus was, Kingdom people are watchful and vigilant—concerning the quality of life, the quality of their own lives, and the presence of God surrounding them. They are prayerful; for it is in the stance and

posture of prayer that the reality of God's reign becomes clearer. People of the Kingdom try, in a world
of individualists, to live a life of local and world community consciousness, for they know God intended
life to be lived in dialogue. Kingdom people are sacramental people, as Jesus was. They know, as Jesus
knew, that the force of *Abba* is unleashed through
tangible signs of faith, hope, and human compassion.
Kingdom people are prophetic and parabolic. We not
only intensely experience the sin and illusions of the
world, we also know in our gut what the world can
be. We prophetically point to that; as a parabolic people we live those possibilities, and therefore indirectly confront and challenge our world.

B) Jesus's Quest

Thomas O'Meara wrote incisively in his *Theology
of Ministry* that a major strain in Christianity has
been, for years, to speak of the evil of the world. Part
of that strain is evident in this book, especially in my
references to the illusions of "consumer spirituality." But Jesus did not intend for his followers to
escape the world in elitist, monastic "groups of the
saved." He intended us to be of, in, and with the
world, actively participating in transforming the
world into the Kingdom of God.

The original Kingdom vision of Jesus had little to
do with the building of basilicas or the establishment
of curias. He came to "light a fire," to begin a revolution of human consciousness and behavior. More
than a static reality, then, the Kingdom is a quest, a
responsibility, a dream. Sunday worship should be

less the cultic, obligatory ritual it often is, and more the Spirit-filled gathering of revolutionaries—not out to overthrow anything, but rather simply trying to help His "Kingdom come," trying to help life be lived as God would have it, not as we, or the forces of evil would have it.

Kingdom people watch the news and read the paper critically. Kingdom members discuss values encased in popular movies, television programs, and music with each other and with their children. Why? Because Kingdom people are as "gentle as lambs, but as cunning as wolves." We have come to the Kingdom only after experiencing the futility of sin. We know the illusions of the age. We walk the streets, enter the work place, intermingle with all of the forces of our age as light, salt, and yeast—trying to lead our world from survival tactics to life in the fullest.

Conclusion

Depth healing for the emotionally troubled can be found in the Kingdom vision of Jesus. The Kingdom outlook on life and the quest for the transformation of the quality of life become life-giving, energizing forces within the person. The quest of the Kingdom is especially helpful for the emotionally troubled. As stated earlier, the emotionally troubled can become pre-occupied with the *self*, forgetting the dialogical nature of life, or concern for people and the world. It is in concern for others that healing awaits the anxious or depressed.

When one becomes part of the Kingdom quest, his or her problems do not magically disappear. Anxiety and depression are frequently chronic syndromes that we must always deal with. Rather than totally eradicating the problems, people who suffer from emotional difficulties carry those wounds with them into relationships and the world. The wounds empower them for greater sensitivity, compassion, acceptance, understanding, and wisdom. As we believe that "by his wounds are we healed," so we believe that our wounds can become a source of new life for others. That is why I wrote this book.

CHAPTER FIVE
Into Your Hands

THE counseling, or therapeutic relationship, was not the only one that I began at the beginning of my anxiety problems. I also began a process of spiritual direction. I had tried spiritual direction before, but I had found it difficult—in one case looking for moral problems to discuss with a director, in another discussing Scripture passages that had no apparent relevance for my life. But in this given year around the campus, spiritual direction was the rage. People pleasing conformist that I was, I contracted to see someone.

The person that I saw was a priest—now a rather famous theologian, speaker, and ministerial consultant on the national scene. His spiritual direction techniques were simple. He encouraged me, and he prayed with me. That notion of encouragement needs some explanation. Encouragement differs from praise. Praise can be strained, at times dishonest. Encouragement, rather, is rooted in reality. It perceives the good and beautiful in a person, and helps reveal it to him or her.

My director truly encouraged me. He would focus on aspects, attributes, gifts present within me that I did not know were there. What I perceived as fatal flaws, he could see as charisms and strengths for ministry. For over twenty years I had struggled to be someone; he simply declared "you are someone; and that someone is truly good."

Such a revelation was truly surprising to me. Someone who has never struggled or never struggled much with feelings of inadequacy finds words like these hard to understand. It is hard for some to understand another person who has feelings of inadequacy or inferiority. Often, to the beholder, they are not understandable; to the person who struggles with them, they are crippling.

Discovering someone who believed in me indeed did encourage me, and helped me to believe in myself. But another piece of input from the spiritual director was more powerful than the encouargement. That was his style of prayer. At each of our sessions, he would invite me to pray.

The only other person I had willingly prayed with was my mother. On some evenings when I was younger, my mother would invite me to join her in the recitation of the rosary. Never had this family custom included spontaneous prayer. The director was beautifully effusive in his emotional prayer style. I would listen, and often envy him. When it came time for me to share my prayer, I was almost ashamed of its simplicity and bare-bones style. All I could do was speak to the Lord what was in my mind and heart at the given moment—sometimes a word of thanks, a hope, a fear, or attitudes of repentance and sorrow. The experience of talking to God from my heart, from the depths of myself became very important to me. Not just in therapy, but also in prayer, I learned how to be totally honest and self-revelatory.

As we closed each evening's sessions, the director prayed the same prayer weekly. He would recite some of the words of Psalm 31, words that Jesus spoke on the cross: "Into Your hands I commend my spirit . . . . O Lord." Those words are interwoven so beautifully with the rest of the psalm.

> In you, O Lord, I put my trust. Let me never
> be put to shame. Deliver me in your righteous-
> ness . . . . You are my rock and my fortress.
> For your name's sake, lead me and guide
> me . . . . You are my strength . . . . Into your
> hands I commend my spirit O Lord. You have
> redeemed me, O Lord God of truth.

My first reaction to the priest's prayer was cynicism. Why was he praying the words of Jesus, dying on the cross. Why the melodrama? But I went along with the show. "Father, into your hands I hand over my life," I would paraphrase.

The model of discipling that we find in the gospels is one that is low on content and high on values. By that I mean the followers of Jesus frequently did not understand the substance of his message, but gradually they caught his values. Such was my experience in this relationship of prayer. I thought the "Into Your Hands" prayer was melodramatic, but I would find myself nonetheless saying it in situations of fear or worry. After reading some things on Eastern mysticism and the practice of mantra praying, or reciting one word or verse over and over again, timed with breathing, I transformed the line into my own Christian mantra. Several times a day I would block a few moments out for an "Into your hands" breather. At times I would focus on part of the prayer and make that my mantra. "Father . . . " I would repeat over and over again on terribly nervous days, trying to break through the cycle of fear to find God. "Into Your Hands," I would repeat on other days when I was obviously causing my own tension by being over-controlling. Finally, I learned to replace the words "my life" with all sorts of people, events, future plans, etc., that caused me bouts of fear and worry. I learned how to prayerfully hand over not only my spirit, but many of the forces that afflicted that spirit.

My spiritual director "discipled," or "mentored" me in a key value of the Kingdom vision of Jesus that my own vision lacked: *trust.* I was the achiever, the controller, the pleaser, the guilt ridden, who often lived life as if I were God. So much anxiety today stems from giving one's heart to the wrong god, or trying to be God one's self. Nouveau-idolatry is so subtle, however. Most of us do not know we are idolatrous. The comfortable routines of religious behavior that we engage in convince us that we are indeed of the Lord. We perpetrate what Luther lamented centuries ago: that religion sometimes allows people to continue in their godless ways.

I recently previewed a docu-drama, made for television, on the growth of cults in America. The program portrayed well the wrenching experience of a young man attracted to a cult-like movement, but caught in the cross-fire of dedication to his family. When a de-programmer was brought in toward the mid-point of the film, the young man revealed the reason for his attraction to the cult: he needed something to believe in. Neither his family experience, nor the culture around him satisfied this hunger and thirst. The cult did. I believe we can find here also the reason for the success of the fundamentalist, evangelical churches that are now attracting so many main-line Catholics and Protestants. We have a built-in need for meaning, purpose, direction, spirituality. So much personal and interpersonal dissonance is due to giving the energy of that need and drive for "what Jesus was about" to our age's golden calves.

The power of prayer is registered in the changed consciousness of the pray-er, as well as in the possible results of prayer, Such was my experience. The "Into Your Hands" prayer—in addition to, but also more than the therapy, began to change my lifestyle, my vision.

Into Your Hands: The Essence of the Kingdom Vision

Consider the man. Mid-thirties. A charismatic personality. He had dedicated his adult life to the sharing of an outlook on life. In the outlook or vision, he believed, was the key to the solution between people and the unhappiness within people. As with so many of us, his career was checkered with both successes and failures. On this particular Friday, he was experiencing the ultimate failure. The very people with whom he had tried to share the vision had rejected him. He was sentenced to the age's version of capital punishment—much more torturous than any of our forms.

As he experienced the ignominy of Roman crucifixion, amid the sun, the insects, the insults of the
crowd, and the depressing undertow of experiencing all of this in view of his mother and people he
dearly loved, there was still within the man an un-
alterable core. Oh, he vacillated. There were moments when he tried to strike a deal: "Father . . . let
this . . . pass . . . . " And there were moments, when
he despaired: " . . . God . . . have You abandoned
me?" But those moments gave way to the "Father
into Your hands" moment.

Jesus's death was a reflection of the way he lived.
He lived "into Your hands." His radical trust in the
midst of crucifixion was, in effect, the beginning of
his resurrection. Easter was in fact contained in seminal form in the Good Friday crucifixion and act of
surrender. Pain was transformed, in an act of faith,
into a passageway toward new life.

The Good Friday scene became for me, in the midst
of my own emotional pain, a reason to go on, a reason
to do more than go on. The "Into Your hands" experience became a *raison d'etre*—a reason for living
and a reason for dying. All living, struggling, suffering, growing, dying, and starting over are part of a
movement toward new life in God. That is what it is
all about—movement toward God. Difficult moments
can become moments of transformation wherein one
can more fully experience the new life of Easter
through our co-operation with the power of God.

"Into Your hands . . . " is a terrible risk. It postulates, or hypothesizes that there is "someone out
there" who cares and will ultimately vindicate good-
ness, truth, and trust. Contained in the words are the

essence of the Kingdom vision of Jesus—at all times, "let go into" the love and Spirit of *Abba*. A point needs to be made here. This is not the "cop-out" approach to life described earlier as "resignation spirituality." Resignation spirituality is passive, expecting God to "do tricks on our behalf." "Into Your hands" spirituality is a co-operative, collaborative spirituality, wherein we, like Jesus, do our part in the transformation of ourselves and our world, and know how to allow God to do his part. "Into your hands" spirituality is an active spirituality in that it engages in an excruciating movement—the relinquishing of the center of our lives to the loving power of God.

Conclusion

"Into Your hands I hand over my life," has become the summary of all of my adult conversions, the one I have shared in this book and the ones that have happened since. At a recent meeting on improving evangelization and ministry in Chicago's Hispanic community, we resolved to try to spark an often overlooked first step. That first step is to encourage Spanish-speaking church-goers to begin a process of prayer for the Hispanic Church in Chicago, and for those who no longer consider themselves part of the Church. We agreed that focused, harnessed prayer would do much more than talks, homilies, or articles in changing the attitudes and consciousness of Spanish-speaking Catholics toward their parishes and those who have become alienated from their Church of origin.

This was my personal experience in praying, mantra-like, the prayer of Jesus on the cross. Many words ago I defined anxiety as the experience of life becoming narrow, of the individual feeling "shut up." Through the power of prayer, a prayer that became as much of my obsessive-compulsive fabric as my fears, a prayer that contained in verbal form the cornerstone of Jesus's lifestyle—radical trust—I began to feel and experience a new power and strength for living, a new expansiveness after years of deepening intraversion. I began to take more risks, to place myself in situations hitherto avoided, but which I now could see were arenas or battlegrounds where the struggle between grace and sinful fear could be fought. Symptoms and anxiety attacks were no longer things to be avoided, but opportunities to be embraced. They could become cross experiences for me, which if experienced within radical trust, could become the beginning of new life, and resurrection for me. I had begun the long road that I am still on —the road of recovery, the journey of conversion, the movement toward God. Some people have such dramatic conversion stories. Mine is a long, plodding, struggling, back-and-forth story. Perhaps disciples will always be plodders.

CHAPTER SIX
Traveling Lightly

AT the heart of Jesus's Kingdom vision is the admonition to live life simply. The Sermon on the Mount, and many other Kingdom discourses call disciples to return life to the simple beauty in which God created it. The person with emotional pain is especially in need of clearing away the clutter of the personal lifestyle to live the simple values of the Kingdom. One of the insights that simplified my life was a verse from the first letter of John, chapter four, verse eighteen. The Johannine author wrote: "There is no fear in love. Perfect love casts out fear . . . . Fear has to do with punishment. Love is not yet perfect in the one who fears."

That brief scriptural quote in many ways sums up everything we have already shared in this book in more technical language. At the root of fear is an absence of love—a depth experience of God's love and also familial and friendship love. The fearful person frequently has never allowed intimacy to happen. It has simplified my life, my periods of struggling with "why do I feel worried or sad right now," to know that often, at the root of it all, is the absence of divine or human love in my life. So often the absence is caused by me, as I pursue the illusions of my own inner commandments and lifestyle.

One John 4:18 has become a kind of a statement of a goal for me. On days of particular emotional pain, I am challenged to practice prayerful surrendering to the God who loves me and wants a closer bond with me. Similarly, I need to stop and look at the roadway littered with eroding relationships, and try to build bridges of reconciliation with those who consistently re-emerge as the ones who care for, accept, and lovingly empower me. The fearful heart is like a growling stomach, longing for food. The food is the indwelling love of the Spirit, and the nurturing love of family and friends.

"Love casts out fear," is a scriptural insight that can simplify and clarify both the cause of and healing for much emotional pain. The person with neurotic struggles also needs some practical skills that perhaps other people do not need to lighten their life journey. I include the skills here, not to add weight to the journey, but to ease the burden of the journey.

1) Patience
Patience is a virtue that becomes a skill for those with emotional problems. As I mentioned in an earlier chapter, we who live in an "instant coffee, microwave world" expect things to happen instantaneously—including our own growth. My thinking has changed on this relative to emotional difficulties. I think now: if it took this long for me to get this way, I'm certainly not going to change it quickly. What matters in the growth from fear and sadness to love, is that one is co-operating with the power of the Spirit in personal transformation. We can no more program growth of the human spirit than we can that of flowers and vegetation. They bloom when they are ready. So also, growth happens when a covergence

of factors—physical, psychological, and spiritual—
"make it happen."

At an Easter vigil, the catechumens (those joining
the Church for the first time) gave some small blooming rose plants to those of us who had helped them
join the Church. The one they gave me was not
blooming at all. The young lady who gave it to me
apologized for its underdeveloped state. As I drove
home, however, I thought that my particular rose
plant was quite appropriate. I did not feel the joy and
new life of Easter at the vigil. I had been in an emotionally dark period all during Holy Week. I did not
have a switch I could turn or a button that I could
press to make myself feel joy and happiness.

I took the rose plant home, and it bloomed a week-
and-a-half later—actually much more appropriately
timed to my own feeling of growth and resurrection.
My point is this: there is no counselor, spiritual
director, or liturgical season that can make us grow.
As a society, we can be so product- or arrival-ori-
ented, that we try to sidestep the process. The only
true growth, however, is growth that has been a process, a process filled with struggles, victories, and
disappointments. We need to learn to appreciate the
journey, not just arriving at our destination.

Neurotic conflicts are much like chronic physical
diseases. They really do not go away. We learn to
temper them, ride the waves with them, laugh during
"up periods," and hold on during stormy periods.
Perhaps the most difficult lesson for the emotional
struggler to learn is that his or her apparently silly and

always annoying emotional conflicts are his or her way of gradually learning how to live the Kingdom.

2) Learning from Setbacks

If you have ever tried to give something up—smoking, eating between meals, drinking, or whatever —you are probably aware of the typical pattern in such efforts. There is the initial period of strong will and ironclad decisiveness, followed by a period of temptation. Many fall during the temptation period. The real struggle is whether, after the fall, can I pick up the pieces, learn from my fall, and move on to continue my therapeutic direction?

Many cave in at the temptation and fall, period. But it need not be such. A "fall" or failure in growth can be a tremendous learning experience in which a person can analyze what led to the diminishing of will power, what he or she needs to do to get back on the road of growth, and then decide again for the therapeutic orientation. The setback can be a powerful learning experience in growing away from addictions or compulsions. The cop-out response, indeed the easiest response to a setback is to throw in the towel—to be defeated by the setback.

This is true also for the growth from fear or sadness. Because of the chronic nature of both syndromes, both anxiety-oriented and depression-oriented persons of necessity go through difficult periods, much like the Holy Week-Easter mood that I described earlier. It is quite easy to throw in the towel during such periods and give in to one's worst perceptions of life and growth. It is so easy to give in to sentiments of "This is the way it is and always will be for me. Why bother? Why try?"

Setbacks can play right into the hands of our own resistance to growth; or, setbacks can become the classroom wherein we learn to understand ourselves better, grow closer to the God of healing and redemption, and strengthen our resolve to continue growth. Setbacks become occasions for praise and thanks that God has supported us and stood by us through painful periods of learning. Setbacks are times to prayfully ask: "Why did that anxiety attack occur? Why did I feel so nervous? So depressed? What was I coming from that might have disturbed me? What was coming up that perhaps might have disturbed me in anticipation? Setbacks are muscle-flexing times—or shipwreck times.

3) Entering Into . . . . Lifting Up

Rachel is a late-thirties mother and wife, who also has a full-time job. The busyness of her life was not the source of her emotional discomfort, however. She seemed to be thriving on activity. Rachel is in her second marriage. Though the second relationship is a healthy, stable one, she has bouts of extreme resentment toward her ex-husband. Visitation days, which he comes to spend with their son, are particularly difficult for Rachel. There is anticipatory anxiety, and then an anger-depression hangover for a couple of days. She came to see me to "get rid of" the anticipatory and hangover feelings.

My advice to her was at first puzzling to her. I told

her that the only way that she could eventually bring some order and tranquility to these painful situations was to enter more deeply into them. When such apparently negative feelings, like anger, or resentment, or anxiety, come our way, we have a culturally conditioned tendency to deny them, or pretend that they are not there. Such "head in the sand" behavior actually perpetuates the very feelings we would like to rid ourselves of. I encouraged Rachel that when she felt anticipatory feelings of anxiety, hurt, anger, or resentment setting in, or the hangover feelings, she need not deny them, but to enter into them.

In the process of entering into our feelings, we prayerfully take time to follow Gendlin's prescription and name the feelings welling up within us. A therapeutically oriented individual is not afraid of or ashamed of any feelings. A person of prayer is willing to stand emotionally naked before God and admit "all that is" within one's self. That demands a great deal of courage for individuals who grew up in a culture that judges certain feelings good and other feelings bad.

Entering into the depth of one's feelings is only the beginning of a process, however. Then, the disciple needs to lift up those feelings in prayer. In the lifting up, the disciple becomes the many people off to the side of the road who called out to Jesus for healing and help. In effect, having entered our painful world, we call out to the Lord, and pray for help and healing in the positive channeling of potentially destructive feelings.

The "lifting up phase" is a courageous entry into

our unreconciled past, an honest experience of our present, and an attempt at a Spirit-filled rehearsal for the future. "Entering into lifting up" is a recognition process, recognition that indeed there are some parts of ourselves that we cannot integrate, heal, or direct effectively just by ourselves. We need a "more than ourselves"—the Lord.

4) Risking

To begin to chart a therapeutic course for one's self is indeed a giant risk. It is a verbal, attitudinal, and behavioral statement that one wants to consciously engage in a process of growth, and a movement toward God. It is risk to leave familiar ways of being and doing in the world to open one's self to learn new ways. It is even a risk to admit one is not in ultimate control of life and to heartfully commit one's self to a lifestyle and discipline of prayer. It is indeed risk to try again, to open one's self to learning after a difficult setback. No one grows who is unwilling to risk. Risk-takers are at least promised the growth of learning. Those who refuse to risk are only assured of the sameness of their life situation.

5) Balancing Small Steps with the Big Picture

I am one of those multi-stimulated people who seems to need to be doing many things at one time. I usually end up "pulling it all off" fairly well. But I cause a lot of havoc for myself and those around me with this tendency. In terms of my own growth, I have the tendency to try to accomplish too much at once. I will read the best books, develop an improved exercise program, deepen my prayer life, and improve my diet—all at once. While I can "pull it all off" in work situations, sometimes I find myself tripping over my own feet when I try multiple efforts at spiritual-emotional growth.

In serving as a counselor for many alcoholics, I learned a key piece of wisdom from one of the therapeutic steps of the Alcoholics Anonymous program—that is, to live one day at a time. Specific to our discussion about growing from anxiety and derpession, those in pursuit of healing and growth need to learn to celebrate small steps taken toward development.

Yet those small steps cannot become a rationale for stagnation. Celebration of small steps needs to be in balance with an eye on the horizon, an eye toward what could be in terms of personal development. The Promised Land of the Old Testament, which offered the Israelites the hope of freedom, liberation, and oneness with each other and their God remains a powerful symbol of intentionality. "What could be" motivates us to trudge, one day at a time, through the dry periods. The dream of the Kingdom replaces illusory intentionality and dreams.

6) Paradoxical Intention

Psychotherapist Victor Frankl discovered something in working with obsessive compulsives and other personality types. It became obvious to him that one of the major difficulties facing such a personality type was what we described earlier as *secondary fear,* or being afraid of being afraid, or being afraid of one's symptoms or condition. It became clear to Frankl that the more a struggling person tried to avoid symptoms, he or she actually could make the condition happen. For example, stutterers could be so afraid that they made the stuttering worse. People prone to anxiety, or panic attacks, could so try to avoid having one that they indirectly make one happen.

Frankl's insight was this: the only way to break the vicious cycle of fear is for the person to "paradoxically intend" the very thing he or she is afraid of. So stutterers have to try to stutter. People with a tendency to anxiety attacks have to try to have one, rather than fret about avoiding having one. Relief from fear can be found in paradoxically intending the thing that is feared the most. In the paradoxical intention there is a perhaps unarticulated conclusion: that which I am afraid of will not seriously harm me; in fact, it is an illusion I have built up in my own head. The person practicing paradoxical intention learns to laugh at the tangled network of primary and secondary fear. In the laughing, the fear-producing situation loses its hold and power over the anxious person. It is almost like an exorcism. Paradoxical intention requires a great deal of courage to practice. It is akin to walking up to the bully, anxiety, and spitting in his face. It does not work if used only once. It needs to be practiced. Gradually, the fear erodes.

Rosemary: An Example

Rosemary is in her early forties. All of her life she

has been plagued by obsessions, compulsions, and guilt. Her presenting symptoms in coming to me recently were a ritualized pattern she goes through in cleaning her house daily, a pre-occupation with sin, and a reluctance to receive the Eucharist because of her perceived moral state. After listening to her stories, I explained to her how many otherwise very intelligent people can get lost in irrational mazes of fear, as she had. I told her I felt her best way out was a disciplined use of paradoxical intention.

We then tried to devise a plan as to what paradoxical intention might look like in her life. We decided she would deliberately clean her house in non-ritualistic ways. She would also force herself to go to communion weekly, without having first celebrated the Sacrament of Reconciliation. The core of the paradoxical intention was this: she would inevitably feel discomfort, guilt, fear of moral condemnation through these two strategies. Her task was to try to feel those uncomfortable emotions, and *then*, not give in to them. The easiest tension-reducing exercise for a person such as Rosemary is to give in to her old rituals. To forgo the rituals and intend the emotional discomfort is indeed crucifixion for her. But there is present in her struggling a conviction that she can break the vicious cycle of fear if she learns to laugh at her fear.

7) *Paradoxical Prayer*

Paradoxical prayer is an energizing complement to paradoxical intention. Paradoxical prayer is rooted deeply in a "Into Your hands" consciousness. It is rooted in the conviction that *Abba* is with us and for us, and that even if our worst neurotic fears are actualized, the God of love will still be with us. In paradoxical prayer, the preliminary conversion of mind and heart needed for paradoxical intention has already taken place. What paradoxical prayer involves is a person of faith, convinced he or she has been swept up in a web of sin and illusion, asking God to allow the situation of discomfort to happen, so that he or she can grow, and continue on the road to freedom. Paradoxical prayer laughs at neurotic fear, and calls on the power of God to help one emerge in the strategy that can exorcise the demons. Paradoxical prayer is rooted in the conviction that God understands the terrors of fear, and wants to be part of the process of liberation.

In paradoxical prayer, people ask God to let the feelings of discomfort come, let the fearful situation happen, let the embarrassing moment take place, let the failure happen. In paradoxical prayer, one even more intently welcomes a face-off with the enemy of fear.

So often, in paradoxical intention and paradoxical prayer, the fearful moment or experience does not "happen," for the conscious intending of the experience prevents the irrational forces that often trigger such experiences from mobilizing. The paradoxical intend-er and pray-er reaches a point where he or she does not care whether the painful moment happens or not, for his or her attention is fixed on *Abba*, into whose hands we are called to surrender.

8) Penetrating Pseudo-Guilt

So often the interior dynamic that gives a person permission to return to neurotic or immature modes of living is that the person feels guilty. It is important to distinguish between real and pseudo-guilt. Real guilt is present when I have done something wrong, and I rightfully feel badly about it. Real guilt is that "programmed in" discomfort we feel when we have violated the values of Jesus or our own best self. Pseudo-guilt is experienced as real guilt. The difference is that it is not rooted in objective wrong. In pseudo-guilt I have violated a neurotic life commandment, a ritual, or compulsion that brings me a false sense of security or relieves neurotic tension. Pseudo-guilt is a force to be reckoned with.

The only way to reckon with it is to use techniques like paradoxical intention, paradoxical prayer, and other comparable techniques wherein one invites in the uncomfortable feelings of pseudo-guilt, praying and struggling all the while for the courage to not give in to them. In other words, the way to break through pseudo-guilt is to paradoxically intend and do the very things that bring on the false feelings of guilt.

9) Humor

The anxious or sad person is morbidly serious, often getting lost in his or her own introspection, and attempts to rid the self of pain. Paradoxical intention, and the other skills related to it, introduce an often overlooked aspect to healing: the importance of humor. Norman Cousins, in his *Anatomy of an Ill-ness*, documents how a self-imposed prescription of funny movies, books, etc., that caused him to laugh heartily each day, significantly contributed to his long-term healing in the face of a serious, chronic ill-ness. The person with neurotic struggles needs not only to laugh at his or her symptoms, but also at himself, and at life. Someone trapped in the past, or trying to control the future, needs to learn how to celebrate the present.

10) Resting
On a particularly stressful day some years ago, I looked to the wall over my desk, and read words from the *Desiderata* poem that had never particularly struck me before. The words are "Many fears are born of loneliness and fatigue." The person with heightened emotional sensitivity needs to be re-minded of how much the physical can play on the emotional—specifically how much fatigue can generate or aggravate fear or sadness. Relative to all the theory and practical advice of this book, no one can go through life always "behaving thera-peutically." We all need breathing space, a time to rest. That rest might involve actual physical resting, or it may involve some other strategy or activity that in the perception of others is not particularly restful. Each person has both a need and a right to define for him or her what is rejuvenating and life-giving.

11) *Claire Weekes's Strategies for Anxiety Attacks*
Perhaps no one has helped people prone to anxiety

attacks more than Claire Weekes. Her books, *Hope and Help for Your Nerves, Peace From Nervous Suffering,* and *Agoraphobia,* offer down-to-earth, common sense approaches to coping with panic attacks. Weekes suggests that trying to avoid or get rid of an anxiety attack actually brings it on, or aggravates one that has already begun.

Her advice, similar in tone to paradoxical intention, is to never run from such an attack, but when it comes, to face it. Facing it, one needs to develop then an attitude of passive nonresistance. One needs to feel all that is happening, without fighting the attack. Fighting makes it worse. The sufferer needs to learn next how to stand his or her ground and let time pass. Anxiety attacks, which seem like they are lasting an eternity, are usually only a few seconds or minutes in duration. Finally, Weekes encourages sufferers to learn how to "float," or pass over to a more peaceful tranquil state of mind and body.

Obviously Weekes' steps are ones that need to be practiced before they become a viable mode of coping for people. Weekes encourages sufferers to be pleased with themselves even if they only take small steps in her process. The small steps gradually move toward a desensitization of anxiety attacks. They happen, but they are not so scarey. Then, they begin to happen less frequently.

12) Compassion

Perhaps the best sense of balance that can be given to one with emotional suffering is to be exposed to the wounds and hurts of others. The size and depth of one's own wounds always seem to diminish in the face of the wounds of others. My opportunity to minister to others often relativizes my own difficulties. All members of the human community have the capacity to enter each other's lives to listen, care, affirm and guide each other. Compassion, or feeling with another, lifts us off of pre-occupation with ourselves. In turn our own periods of internal struggle and conflict more acutely sensitize us to the pain of other people. Because we have struggled, we see the struggle in others, understand it, and are empowered to "be with another" more effectively.

Conclusion

Kingdom living is about living simply in and through the power of the Spirit. Sometimes Kingdom simplicity is so elusive for us in the computer age that it becomes complex. Kingdom people try to carry as little baggage as possible, but Kingdom people with problems, with fear or sadness, need to carry a few extra light tools around with them—just in case.

Some of the above attitudes and behaviors are quite effective for "putting out emotional fires," as they begin, and after they have begun. Someone interested in genuine growth needs to do more than put out fires. He or she needs to create a therapeutic, healthy climate or milieu in which genuine growth can take place. We now turn our attention to what such a growth-oriented life ecology might look like.

CHAPTER SEVEN
Developing a Spiritual Program

DURING my first few years as a priest, the themes of my preaching attracted a good number of people who were recovering from alcoholism or drug addiction. Frequently such a person wanted a trustworthy objective party with whom they could do a moral inventory—a catharsis-like releasing of some of the sin and flaws of one's past and present life. In ministering to and interacting with many people from Alcoholics Anonymous and other therapeutic processes modeled on A.A., I began to pick up a key insight from their strategy for healing. Once an alcoholic, for example, has had some seminal experience of the "Higher Power," or healing Mystery, that brings sobriety, he or she must arrange the pieces of daily life so that the healing event is daily retrieved, experienced anew, and deepened. The recovering addict needs to maintain "daily, conscious contact" with that Higher Power. To do that, a person needs to develop a daily spiritual program.

One of the things that has consistently impressed me about the A.A. notion of the spiritual program is that it insists on the necessarily unique nature of each person's program. In an age when the Body of Christ yearns for the computer printout that will insure personal conversions and ongoing parish renewal, A.A. speaks of the importance of each person finding the spiritual program that is uniquely right for him or her.

I spoke recently to a group of people who had experienced the trauma of divorce. In the course of the talk, I tried to share some of the things that have become important pieces of my spiritual program. After the presentation, I asked for reactions to some of the suggestions I had made about steps in a spiritual program. Many of the people resonated with what I had spoken about and suggested. One woman, however, spoke up and probably expressed the feelings of other, more timid group members. She said that she found some of my techniques terribly introspective. She mentioned that, especially when she felt anxious or depressed, she needed to reach out to someone to share feelings with, rather than engage in activity that brought her increasingly into her core.

The woman's reactions have stayed with me, because I think she unconsciously articulated a key insight into the spiritual malaise, or drifting, of many Christian people. Much of both the Catholic and Protestant worlds speak as if there is but one way to experience God. Some claim that is found in compulsive Scripture study; others that the answer is in monastic prayer styles. Others hold onto the traditional values of Sunday worship and the developmental celebration of sacraments. Many of the forms of spiritual expression and development, popular in America, have been introverted or competitive models, in which the individual finds God privately through personal struggle and prayer.

The divorced woman was simply saying, "I'm a more extroverted person; I find God in relationships with others." Adrian Van Kaam has spoken and written extensively about the *unique* spiritual direction that each human life must follow. Spiritual direction is the unfolding of the best and true self that I am meant to be. As there are certainly a plurality of types of selves, so also there must be a plurality of styles of actualizing the self and touching the God who energizes and empowers that self.

William Glasser, the father of *Reality Therapy*, puts it another way. In a book entitled *Positive Addictions*, Glasser speaks of how in contemporary society many of us fall prey to negative addictions. *Negative addictions* are those compulsions, obsessions, and habits that creep into our lives and rob us of life rather than help us to experience what Jesus said he came to give us—full life. Positive addictions, on the other hand, are *do's and don'ts* that I practice daily that create that context, or milieu, spoken of in the last chapter, which is oriented toward full life rather than coping or survival. In the development of positive addictions, what works for one might not work for another.

I intend this chapter to be kind of smorgasbord, or an offering of a few words on many different pieces of spiritual programs that are proving helpful for many different types of people. In no way is this presentation exhaustive or all-inclusive. I mention these positive addictions, or pieces of a potential spiritual program, as a way of "priming the pump," to generate the readers' creativity in naming, being affirmed in, or planning for their own spiritual program. These "pieces" also strive to strike a balance between introverted and extroverted spirituality.

1) Solitude

In a world of techno-stress, nuclear threat, and the inevitable push and pull of our own life commandments, we all need time for solitude and quiet. Aloneness is the environment in which listening to our own deepest selves, to the cries of the wounded world, and to the call of God can take place. "Being your own best friend," which the culture and pop therapies of the age encourage us to be, involves more than immediately gratifying every internal impulse. It means spending time with ourselves, and getting to know ourselves intimately, just as we need to spend time with others to get to know them intimately. Solitude involves our assuming the posture we would in growing in awareness of anyone else: that is, a posture of listening, of letting go of some of our pre-occupation to enter into our own inner realm and to enter more deeply into compassion for the world.

Solitude that leads to prayerful contemplation is a wasting of functional, productive time, a letting go of some of life's problems, to experience more fully life's mysteries, and the Mystery. Solitude is not a one-shot experience for a retreat, or a once-in-a-while experience. Solitude needs to become a discipline for the person seeking inner peace. Solitude is the threshold for many of the healing experiences and techniques mentioned in this book.

2) Togetherness

A recent study on the dynamics that lead up to

marital infidelity revealed that one contributing factor in the erosion of a marriage is the fact that so many men let go of male friends upon getting married, and then often do not develop new friendships. Work, achievement, and finances crowd out the time and energy needed to form lasting friendships. Frequently "together time" is a rare occurrence in most marriages. Marital relationships become functional and utilitarian. Yet the void left by the absence of intimacy cries out to be filled. The absence of ongoing friendships and intimacy in marriage are significant factors in the infidelity pattern.

Anxious, stressful, depressed people are often lonely people, shut up and isolated in their own inner chaos or confusion. Alfred Adler had as one of his cornerstone ideas the notion of *social interest*. *Social interest* was Adler's way of speaking of life as it should be lived. Social interest refers to an orientation toward people and relationships. Such an orientation, for Adler, was a sign of health and normalcy. Adler felt that people with neurotic and psychotic difficulties had "underdeveloped social interest." They so much respond to their own inner dictator, or life commandments, that they fail to develp loving and lasting relationships. Adler saw lack of social interest as a global concern. To the degree both individuals and nations are motivated by competition, power, and superiority, to that same degree are we non-cooperative with each other, and disinterested in relationships.

People with emotional difficulties need to decide again, or for the first time, about the value of relationships. *Friendship*, with the same sex, with the other sex, and "marriage as an intense form of friendship" need to be re-discovered as signs of emotional health, and signs also of gospel living. The experience of love and friendship and the encouragement, challenge, and support that come with them are vital forces for healing emotional wounds. The healing occurs, not only in the gratification of being loved, but also in the experience of learning how to love.

3) *Balancing Activity and Rest*

I already briefly commented on the importance of rest for the emotional sufferer. I would like to briefly expand on it. I have a point that I reach, which I have never really shared with anyone before. I call it the "I have to get this boy to bed" period. Occasionally, I reach a point where none of the techniques that we have shared work in alleviating emotional pain. I know now such periods are the result of overwork and fatigue. The person interested in emotional growth and wholeness needs a discipline about balancing activity and rest. Learning this discipline is extremely difficult for one personality type especially prone to anxiety, that is the obsessive-compulsive, the overly responsible person who always needs to be active and productive.

Rest is a term that needs some explanation. The author of the Letter to the Hebrews speaks of *God's rest* as a spiritual reality or consciousness that we can enter into and participate in. For the author, rest is a state of oneness and communion with God, begun here and continued in the afterlife. *Rest* sometimes necessarily involves physical inactivity and sleep. The psalmist writes about how fruitless much of our activity is and how God blesses us through rest and sleep. But sleep is a deceptive thing, and can also become the "escape route" for many anxious or depressed people seeking to anesthetize their pain or avoid therapeutic activity that touches on their core conflicts.

Rest is more than sleep. Rest includes recreation, or more accurately *re-creation*. The emotionally struggling person usually has underdeveloped talents, abilities, or interests. He or she frequently has never been helped to name his or her personal gifts, or shown activities in which those gifts could be used. In developing a spiritual program, a person needs to give serious consideration to the importance of rest, recreation, and the need for re-creation. A person needs to be honest, and noncompetitive in naming what is genuine restful recreation for his or her unique personality.

4) A Variety of Styles of Prayer
A) Spontaneous Prayer

An elderly man approached me recently to speak about difficulty in prayer. As he tries to "say his prayers," he finds a kind of tug-of-war present within him in which his authentic self wants to go in one direction, and his praying self feels there is a pre-set direction he ought to be following.

The man seemed a bit scandalized when I gave him my definition of prayer, that is, "standing naked before God." If prayer is anything, it needs to be a time when I can totally be myself in the presence of God. If I am really to be myself, it is fictive to think I, or anyone for that matter, is always this way, or never that way. Totally being myself involves times of worry, guilt, joy, praise, repentance, and on and on. For the anxious person, prayer can become a time to share some of the things that I am worried about, no matter how irrational or silly they appear to be. For the stressful person, prayer can become a preview of the challenges ahead and an invitation to God to be a partner in the challenge. For the depressed person, prayer can be a naming of the wounds, or the demons that are tugging down the spirit.

While structured prayer, or disciplined prayer, is sometimes what is most needed for an individual, the person with emotional pain can derive great benefit from learning to pray personally, honestly, to be one's self before God. Such prayer is a real test of whether an individual believes in the essence of Jesus' Abba spirituality. If I really believe in the loving someone who accepts and forgives me, as well as challenges me, I will seek out moments of intimacy with that personal, loving force. To avoid such personal prayer is sometimes a sign that God lives in my head, but not yet in my heart and my lifestyle. The late Karl Rahner used to say that many of us remain superficial and impersonal in prayer because we know that opening ourselves to depth intimacy with God might lead us in directions that we do not necessarily want to go.

There is in personal, spontaneous prayer great potential, not only for challenging new directions in one's life, but also radical healing. At a recent seminar that I conducted on coping with suffering, I asked participants what helped them in their moments of pain. One woman spoke up and said it was personal, spontaneous prayer from the depth of her ache, the depth of her spirit, that healed her.

Three passages especially stand out for me as clear articulations of the healing power of prayer: in Mark 9, the disciples are wondering why they could not heal a possessed boy, as Jesus did. Jesus replies, "This kind (of demon) you can only drive out with prayer." There are parts of my emotional world that I know I cannot heal by myself. I know because I have tried. An ongoing process of naming our emotional wounds, entering into them rather than running from them, and inviting the God of courage and healing into those wounds is needed for genuine healing of minds and spirits. Francis MacNutt and others have written extensively on this phenomenon.

The eleventh chapter of Luke throws further light on the healing power of prayer. In the 13th verse, after encouraging the disciples to "ask . . . seek . . . and knock," Jesus identifies the real "pay-off" in prayer. " . . . The . . . Father gives the Holy Spirit to those who ask him." Luke's version is a change from the parallel passage in Matthew in which Jesus says the Father gives "good things" to those who ask him. Luke identifies the source of the healing power of prayer. For the emotional sufferer, "good things" are not as important as knowing "the Spirit" is with you. Prayer is our deliberate paying attention to that loving, life-giving Spirit.

In Matthew 5:44-45, Jesus speaks the revolutionary challenge to "pray for enemies." Prayer for enemies is an example of something I referred to earlier in the book as "paradoxical prayer." Whether we are praying for enemies or those who have hurt us, or praying that God allow us to feel the pain of a neurotic symptom that we might eventually grow desensitized to it, prayer is an exercise in exploding the status quo of our lives, to experience some of what Jesus meant by new life, freedom, and resurrection. Prayer is the experience not so much of measurable results in life, as of our hearts gradually changing. In paradoxical prayer, my spirit or my consciousness is altered.

Prayer is indeed the language of conversion and the transformation of the imagination. Along the shore of Lake Michigan, on the near north side of Chicago, where I jog daily, I see so many young people biking, running, skating or sunning with their transistorized stereos hanging on their belts and headphones in their ears. Most are listening to their favorite music. Perhaps I am old fashioned, or getting to the point where I just want to have quiet when I run, but I wonder about the urgency some of them feel to have noise even in the midst of recreation. The new miniature units with headphones further isolates the individual; he or she does not even have to attend to the people that they are recreating with. More relevant to our topic, the individual imagination is muted or anesthetized. The isolating, privatized music, and values and images contained in the music, do the imaging for the person.

Rather than dominating or overpowering the human spirit or imagination as seems to happen in the above situation, prayer is a merging of spirits, a communion of imaginations. My internal symbols, frames of reference, myths are welded to God's as revealed through Jesus. At once, prayer jars and challenges my internal world and affirms and encourages other parts of it.

B) Prayer for the Past, Present, and Future

Healing prayer is temporally oriented. When we turn to God for healing, we usually have an eye toward our past, present, or future. Much psychic pain flows from something repressed or unresolved in the past, something erupting in the present, or something looming on the horizon of the future. In healing prayer we enter our past, present, and/or future in communion with God.

Prayer for the Past

Tom is an able young man in his mid-twenties, with an interest and talent for writing and journalism. Tom came to see me because of his "string of back luck" with jobs. No job lasted more than two years for him. His superficial analysis of his situation was that fate consistently dealt him a bad hand in the bosses that he had. As we talked more, Tom and I came to see that he had trouble with any male in an authority position over him. Some of the faults of his supervisors were quite real. But he brought his own problems to those relationships because of his own relationship with his father.

Tom's father was an alcoholic. He grew up in a home in which the environment was quite unpredictable. Tom never knew whether a paternal hand stretched toward him would pat his cheek or knock him off the chair at the dining room table. Tom had unresolved conflicts with his father that he transferred over to or projected on anyone in authority. The reason that he could never compromise with a boss was because through them he was expressing the repressed rage he felt toward the father who provided him with such an unstable foundation for life and relationships.

Therapy has involved teaching Tom to use his memory, imagination, and attention to enter into those hurting memories—to see them again, name the hurt and then lift the hurt up to the Lord in prayer. Tom's repeated prayer became: "Heal the pain and anger I have toward my father. Bless him with health and happiness. Teach me to love him, despite what has gone on in our past lives." Months of such prayerful remembering, imagining, and attending have begun—I stress the word begun—to soften Tom's anger. Beginning to be freed from his past, he approaches others, especially authority figures, differently.

For any of us with unresolved emotions from the past, healing can be found in using memory, imagination, attention, and prayer to "enter into . . . see . . . name . . . and lift up." Again this is a process rather than a moment or an event.

Prayer for the Present
I recently had a day-long meeting with a priest

from the West Coast, whose full time ministry is to represent his diocese on television, radio, and other media. He openly confessed before our group, that he still becomes very nervous as he waits to do such events. He has developed a therapeutic strategy for himself, however. For five minutes before an appearance or interview, wherever he is, he goes into the bathroom. He closes the door of the room (or stall) and quiets himself down. Then he pays attention to the Spirit of God with him. Rather than praying for success, he tries to center himself on, or anchor himself, in the presence or Spirit of God. Most often he performs with peace and confidence because of his "prayer for the present."

I have had many such experiences before preaching or speaking. It is not the experience of "praying for a home run," but rather the experience of realizing unconditional love is really with us. In my case, such centering or anchoring releases an energy in me, a freedom, a realistic self-confidence. Use of attention and prayer in the present clears away the anxious, stressful clutter within and around us. We remember who we really are, and what we are about.

Prayer for the Future

Agnes, like Rachel in an earlier chapter, came to see me because of anxiety she had around "visitation days," days when her ex-husband came to pick up their son for a day together. About two days before his visit, Agnes begins to feel anxious, to "feel small" in comparison to him and other people. For several days afterward, she would have an anger hangover that troubled her.

I suggested that Agnes begin listening to herself, naming some of her feelings, and then do something to transform those feelings into growth. Specifically I asked her to begin rehearsing for the future through the use of memory, imagination, attention, and prayerful entering into and lifting up. I shared with Agnes that there are many situations in my own life that cause me fear, anger, stress, and a variety of other painful emotions—just in my anticipating them. Rather than waste energy in fear and anxiety, or run from them in my own imagination, I now emotionally and spiritually enter into my future with God.

For other situations in which I know I might be judgmental, intolerant, impatient, or uncharitable, I try to discern what would be a proper discipleship stance toward people or events, and ask God to help me be or do what will be appropriate for Kingdom living. Prayer is rehearsing for life and the future with God. Such a prayer style radically tempers fear about the future.

C) Summary: Prayer is . . .

I have spent a lot of time and space on prayer because I believe it is the language of conversion, the re-imaging of our internal frames of reference, our appropriation of Jesus' Kingdom consciousness. To round out this presentation, I would like to make a descriptive list of what prayer is.

Prayer is . . .

> *time:* my whole life is not a prayer, as the wisdom of the 60's said; rather my life can

be prayerful, if I make time to pray.

words: whether spoken in the imagination, out loud, or written, we need to incarnate our thoughts and feelings in words; articulation contributes toward healing.

silence: as stated in earlier sections on solitude and listening, sometimes we just need to be quiet to better create an environment for prayer and learning.

music and environment: sights, sounds, and smells around me can create an intuitive feeling of God's presence.

self-awareness: in prayer I can be my total, honest, self with God.

awareness of others: maturing prayer moves off of the self to compassion for others, and concern for the global community.

an act of God: prayer allows the Spirit to move through and influence our lives.

an act of a person: in prayer we alternately initiate or respond in relationship to God.

an act of love: in prayer, we enter into intimacy with God, bringing with us all whom we love.

an act of hope: to even begin to pray is to give evidence of a belief in and hope for a Someone who loves and cares.

communication: much like the sharing of thoughts and feelings in other love relationships, prayer is a sharing of our inner worlds with God and a listening for his self-disclosure.

an act of faith: to reach out to God in prayer
is behavior that flows from a previous decision—commitment; that decision is a leap of
the thinking and imagining processes that the
mystery at the center of life is personal and
loving.

an experience of solidarity: serious prayer
unites one's own pain and struggle with that
of Jesus and the rest of struggling humanity
around the world.

an experience of Church: Avery Dulles, in
both *Models of Church* and *A Church to
Believe In*, has reminded us that one of the
many dimensions of Church is the experience
of mystical communion with God; in prayer
we experience one of the essential elements
of life in the Body of Christ.

practicing Kingdom consciousness: in prayer,
I let go of some images and metaphors of
my own private logic, the consumer culture
around me, and other forces and influences,
to dwell in metaphors and images of the
Kingdom; prayer, then, is practicing the
Kingdom consciousness of Jesus.

the language of love and conversion: as shared
thoughts and feelings are the indicators of
developing intimacy between marriage
partners and friends in general, so also a
prayerful life is an expression of deepening
communion with God and an indicator of the
mystery of conversion of heart, mind, and
behavior happening with progressive
intensity and profundity within us.

5) Eucharist

After a Sunday Eucharist recently, a worshipper came up and expressed gratitude for the celebration. It was one of those times when everything worked well together—homily, choir, lectors. Most of the congregation, including myself, were really into the experience. The man who came up to comment afterward said, "Gee, I wish every Sunday were like this, I feel as if I were at a pep rally."

We cannot expect every Sunday liturgy to be like a pep rally in terms of level of enthusiasm and effect. The pep rally image, however, more accurately captures the meaning of Eucharist than the staid lifeless rituals experienced in so many Catholic parishes, as well as Protestant churches celebrating the Lord's Supper. Sunday is a time for Kingdom people to gather to re-commit themselves to the revolution, the revolution of Jesus.

I made this last comment at a Eucharist preparation evening for parents at a rather conservative parish in Chicago. When I referred to believers as a group of revolutionaries who refuse to buy into the values of the age, and the Eucharist as a time for us revolutionaries to re-commit ourselves to the cause and to Jesus, I aroused cynicism and antagonism in some of my listeners. Many there that evening still saw Eucharist as a private, personalized act of devotion between the self and God.

For the person struggling emotionally, the Eucharist is an experience of remembering the values of the Kingdom, values and attitudes that are at variance with the anxiety-producing and depression-prone values of private logic or contemporary culture. Being reminded of those values through the Word, we are invited to decide again for them, re-commit to them. We share the struggle to take on the mind of Christ with fellow worshippers, who are there with their own tension of Kingdom living ver-sus illusion. By being together, we are reminded that the transformation of the world into the Kingdom of God, and the transformation of our own personal lives toward the Kingdom cannot be done alone. As Braxton says in the *Wisdom Community:* we need each other to experience life as ever deepening mystery rather than a series of problems. Finally, at the Eucharist the life-giving presence of God, in the shared faith of the assembly and in the sacramental signs of bread and wine, become real "food and drink" for the journey of life.

In short, the Eucharist reminds us of who we should be. It challenges us to let go of that which keeps us from Kingdom living. It feeds us, supports us toward that end. But that "it" of the Eucharist is not a thing, but the commingling of faithful so-journers and the Spirit of God all moving toward the victory of Resurrection. Without the Eucharist as part of one's spiritual program, a person can forget who and what we are called to be. Another equally dangerous extreme is to make the Eucharist into one's whole spiritual program. The Eucharist is an extremely important piece, but it cannot provide for all aspects of spiritual growth. It needs to be joined to a selection of other healing, therapeutic activities.

6) Bibliotherapy

I use a rather technical term here to refer to the immense help that reading can bring to one in pursuit of growth. Some people who by nature are drawn to words and thoughts rather spontaneously respond to helpful reading materials. In fact, reading has proven to be a source of help for all types. Scripture, books of a psychological nature, books of a spiritual or theological nature, all can both provide new information and insights to the emotional struggler, as well as help him or her realize that the pain of anxiety, stress, or depression is not unique to them. Therapeutic reading informs, edifies, and supports.

7) Diet and Exercise

In our compartmentalized living, we often do not connect eating styles or physical activity to the spiritual life. Yet if many of us harken back to our childhood, we can at least remember fasting and abstinence from meat as ultimately tied up with spiritual living. Recent research into *anorexia nervosa* and *bulimania* (binging and purging cycles) reveal how food is often symbolically connected to the core of one's personal and interpersonal issues. Research has also confirmed that eating more or eating less frequently are connected to periods of anxiety, stress, or depression.

Food, eating, and drinking are an important part of living. They are indeed connected with our psychic selves. If spirituality is in part a process of "becoming whole," then spirituality and one's spiritual program must also take into account the issues of food and drink. A person seeking spiritual wholeness makes as part of a spiritual program a diet that insures optimum nutrition, weight, and vitamin-

chemical balance. Such "nouveau-asceticism" requires a discipline of both mind and body. The discipline is not motivated by the youth culture: "I'll go
through this pain to try to regain the body of an
adolescent or look good on the beach." Rather the
motivation is deeply spiritual: "I want to respect this
gift of life God has given me. I want to participate
in optimum balance and collaboration between my
physical self and my emotional, spiritual self." By
way of negative summary, so often people who report a lot of nervousness or sadness are also found to
have unhealthy eating habits.

Fasting can be of value in moving toward emotional health. For the neurotic, however, fasting can
become a danger—another outlet for obsession or
compulsion. Fasting is best used on an occasional
basis as a way of purifying the physical systems, and
as a kind of progressive ongoing prayer of consciousness raising or attending to the presence of God and
all the suffering people of the world.

Talk of diet leads naturally to a consideration of
exercise. Because of childhood illness, I did not
develop a lot of skills in competitive athletics, except
for basketball, which I only occasionally and momen-
tarily partake in for fear of a massive coronary.
About eight years ago, I experimented with jogging.
If you remember, in the mid-seventies, much was
written about the benefits of running. I was re-inforced by the writing of William Glasser (*Reality
Therapy, Positive Addictions*), who has written and
lectured extensively on both the bio-chemical and

consequent emotional change that are a direct result of running.

For years I have been a cluster headache sufferer. While migraines seem to befall women more frequently than men, and are located toward the front of the head, clusters seem to affect men more frequently and are located in the back and sides of the head. Whether migraine or cluster, the net result is the same—excruciating and nauseating pain. Over the years, I have tried most remedies, but most convinced me that you just had to wait out a headache, almost like a thunderstorm passing through.

During an agonizing and fitful night and early morning with a headache several years ago, I decided to do something completely irrational. I decided to jog—at three in the morning. Though I feared being reported to the police, I tried it. The pain of running with a headache, for about five minutes, was awful. Then I began to notice something: the pain on the right side of my head began to lessen. I could sense my heart and blood pulsating in a different way. The headache was gone.

When I get a headache now, I go jogging—much to the puzzlement of family and friends. My experience with tension headaches and their remedy through jogging has convinced me of the inter-connectedness between mind and body. I have felt re-inforced recently by research that shows some forms of headaches do indeed respond to chemicals released into the bloodstream by jogging.

Lest I be misconstrued as waging a campaign for

jogging, I am simply trying to re-state and re-empha-
size the importance of physical activity—joined to
prayer, Eucharist, reading and diet control—as a
means of growth toward wholeness. Personalities
are so different! Each person must discover the
physical activity that works for him or her. Some re-
tain the physical stamina for competitive sports (like
raquetball or basketball). Others like the noncompetitive context of jogging. Still others like
calisthenics or aerobics. Others prefer the tranquil,
yet rigorous experience of walking.

There is no "golden calf" exercise program. Each
individual has to find one that fits. Jogging provides
me with an opportunity to not only stimulate the cardiovascular system, but also "think about nothing
and everything" for fifteen to twenty minutes. It is an
important retreat time for me. As one progresses in a
physical component to one's spiritual program, there
is a real feeling of discomfort (both physical and
emotional-spiritual) if it is omitted.

8) Journaling - Dreams - Memories

In the section on listening, I tried to emphasize the
therapeutic value of listening to the self and naming
issues, feelings, and conflicts within. As Eugene
Gendlin has suggested in his *Focusing* book and exer-
cises, so much of the inner self goes unnoticed or
unattended. In that process of becoming a listening
person, journaling can become an important instru-
ment. Journaling is the written account of one's
inner journey. As Ira Progoff has pointed out in his
journaling books and seminars, journaling can pro-

vide an opportunity to simply document one's inner experiences, or to address, in an authentic fashion, significant people or experiences from the past. Whatever form it takes, journaling helps in the naming and catharsis process.

I use journaling to commune with the ground of my becoming, God. In short prayerful passages, I lift up unreconciled past events, painful current emotions, or anxiety-producing future events.

In journaling, there are two phenomena to remain especially aware of: dreams and memories. Dreams are looked on by those of a psychoanalytic orientation as the reservoir or deposit of unresolved conflicts and emotions. On the other hand, Adlerians see dreams as a factory of emotions for the future. In other words, in dreaming we are preparing, rehearsing for future conflicts and issues that we know we must soon address. I believe the truth to be somewhere in the middle between Freudians and Adlerians. Dreams are an expression of past, present, and future issues. With a trusted guide, we need to pay attention to and interpret them. In journaling, we can record them.

So also, we can record memories—specifically spontaneous memories that become important to us. Alfred Adler believed spontaneous memories to be very important in therapy. In short, we remember for a reason. At the root of people's memories is a perceptual system that remembers certain things for a reason. Get to the person's perception system via memories, and you have begun to unravel the mystery of a person. Frequently, both Adler and

Rudolf Dreikers felt, growth can be registered in a chronicling of changing spontaneous memories. Memories, like dreams, can be studied, talked about, and prayed through if they are written down.

A) *Moral Inventory and the Experiences of Reconciliation*

Life would be easy if the mystery of evil were as simple as traditional moral manuals would have us believe. As the great harmartiology, or study of sin, in chapters 3-11 of *Genesis* indicate, sin is, in fact, quite subtle in its presence in most of our lives. Sin lurks in unreflected-upon, knee-jerk-like attitudes, values, and approaches to things.

Emotional difficulties themselves can be a sign of selfishness or irresponsibility, or an attempt to avoid dealing with one of the life tasks. When one discloses such a pattern within one's self, it indeed becomes a matter of morality whether one addresses it or not. One of the main ideas running through this book is that what we leave unnamed within us frequently becomes a demonic force within us. So it is with sin. Both Karl Menninger in *Whatever Became of Sin* and M. Scott Peck in *People of the Lie* have written of the self-deception involved in the contemporary age's rationalization of evil.

A.A. makes one of the main features of its spiritual steps the experience of a fearless moral inventory on one's self and the sharing of that moral self analysis with another person. I suggest that moral inventories are an important part of emotional and spiritual healing for anxious and depressed persons as well. Moral inventories and experiences of reconciliation challenge the emotional struggler to live out of a morality that is indeed Kingdom oriented. The person is challenged regularly to scrutinize the personal degree of responsiblity for the gift of life.

Experiences of reconciliation may take on the familiar trappings of Catholic sacramental life. They may also be found in depth discussions with a therapist, or the real, existential sharing of thoughts, feelings, hurts, and forgiveness with a significant other. Most important for our purposes, a person growing emotionally is trying to live honestly, emotionally, and peacefully with the people in his or her life.

10) Therapeutic Goals

As Theodore Issac Ruben in *Reconciliation: Inner Peace in an Age of Anxiety* has pointed out, most of us are in pursuit of something outside of ourselves as the perceived key to satisfaction and happiness. In the pursuit of the "mythical it," we set goals and objectives for ourselves that seem to lead to success and happiness.

Part of a therapeutic spiritual program involves a change in the style of goal-setting. A person begins to see that it is not setting goals for the control and manipulation of the external world but rather goal-setting for the internal, psychological, spiritual world that leads to true happiness. Such a renewed approach includes making new friends, developing hobbies, discovering new recreational forms, learning new styles of prayer, and other related activities as targets for meaningful goal-setting. Such goals lead one to a re-directed course of growth—from upward mobility to deepening personality integration.

11) Ministry

This is a development of a seminal thought from the previous chapter, that is, my reference to compassion. My own spiritual program would not be complete if I did not include the therapeutic value of learning to care for others. As the twelfth step of A.A. indicates, health can be found in helping another. Baptism calls each person to serve or minister. It is our pre-occupation in the Catholic Church with Holy Orders ministry and our mindlessness toward Baptismal ministry that keeps our Church from true renewal and evangelical greatness.

The chaotic lay volunteerism of the past 20 years is not true ministry. Ministry involves a discernment of gifts, or one's share in the Holy Spirit, and a using of those gifts for others and for the glory of God. When an emotional sufferer engages in such other-centered activity, the chains of anxiety or depression begin to be broken.

Conclusion

This list of ingredients for a spiritual program is not meant to be exhaustive. Neither am I implying that the use of all of what I have suggested insures an effective spiritual strategy for all readers. The spiritual program is a phenomenon that needs to be uniquely devised by the individual. Most often it involves several key elements that help the individual keep body, intellect, emotions, and spirit in harmony.

The spiritual program is a discipline—a regular routine of *do's* and *don'ts* that keeps one kind to the self, rooted in God, and reconciled to one's fellow person. What keeps a person on such a therapeutic track? What prevents a person from returning to old ways of feeling, thinking, and believing? Each of us needs to be rooted in what we believe to be the meaning of life. It is a person's meaning system that maintains motivation and energy for the spiritual program. I believe the "meaning of it all" is found in the words "life, death, and resurrection." We turn to that reality in the next chapter.

CHAPTER EIGHT
Paschal Living

AS I drive from the southwest suburban area of the Chicago metropolitan area into the center of the city, I am always struck by the Chicago skyline, which looms on the horizon on a clear day. The Sears Tower, the Hancock Building, the Standard Oil Building stand majestically as statements of the power of human ingenuity and creativity. But on some days, these buildings activate a Biblical archetype within me. I look at them and think of the Tower of Babel, that symbol of both will power and ability, as well as the human family's capacity for chaos, confusion, and alienation. I also am reminded of how such monuments to ourselves seem to deny a central issue of human living—that we are limited, vulnerable, mortal creatures. All of the architecture, science, and progress that seem to boast of who we are and what we can do seem to gloss over the awesome fact that each of us must die.

I remind the reader of Otto Rank's theory that most anxiety can be traced back to discomfort over the issues of separation or death. Ernest Becker wrote incisively in the *Denial of Death* about how much of contemporary busyness and activity is an attempt to not deal with one's own personal mortality. One has not really reached maturity until he or she has in some way faced, reached some conclusions about, and emotionally integrated the reality of death.

My purpose in concluding this volume with a reflection on death is my own conviction that there is no true and lasting growth without an experience of death. There is no appropriation of a new consciousness or vision about life without a willingness to let go of another one. There is no experience of new values and new behavior without a real struggle and period of crucifixion. There can be no life without a willingness to die. The person who is anxious, stress-filled, or depressed will find no relief if she or he is unwilling to die in a variety of different ways.

Jesus and Death

I find great comfort in the account of Jesus' last hours, because he does not exhibit univocal courage, but rather a variety of different emotions. I see a pattern in Jesus' experience of Holy Thursday night and Good Friday.

1) He allows himself to feel many different emotions about death: denial, attempts at bargaining with his Father (denial), anger (at his disciples' diffidence and apathy), fear, and sadness. The Scriptures depict him entering into those feelings and experiencing them intensely.

2) The variety of emotions do not trigger a retreat pattern on the part of Jesus. With the ambiguity of differing emotions, he faces and confronts the moment of death.

3) Whenever a writer tries to explain a process, he or

she oversimplifies as if life unfolds in clear stages. Our grids and flow charts are only poor attempts at objectifying mystery. As I speak about Jesus' approach as paradigmatic for us, I also write in stages, but my stages are only an attempt at giving a simplified picture of something that is essentially mysterious. As Jesus *felt*, and *faced*, there was an additional perduring emotional-spiritual tone—that of *surrender*. The scriptures suggest that shot through Jesus' very human emotional bouncing there was an immutable conviction: that Abba, the Father of love, was with him and would be with him in a passage from the moment of defeat to an experience of new life.

4) The Good Friday articulation of Jesus' inner core, "Father into Your Hands I commend My Spirit," was actually the beginning of Easter Sunday. More than days, or temporal events, Good Friday-Easter Sunday represents an attitude toward life. That attitude consists of: a willingness to face the discomfort involved in growth, an honesty about all the emotions involved in that discomfort, a spirit of cooperation and surrender with Abba who assures us of always being with us with his love, and the felt experience of passing over into new life.

The apparent internal experience of Jesus in facing death is a model for those of us seeking emotional-spiritual growth: to face, feel surrender, and gradually emerge into new life.

Passage Spirituality

The title of this chapter, "Paschal Spirituality," needs to be translated. *Paschal spirituality* simply refers to the passage nature of life and growth. It refers to the passage orientation of Jesus' vision of life, indeed the passage nature of Old Testament faith. In the Old Testament, the people of God were always in transition. In the New Testament, the disciples of Jesus are always described as in movement, on a journey. The systems of spirituality or philosophies of the spiritual life that speak of spirituality in static terms or idealize about a perfection or a status quo that can or will be eventually reached really contradict the passage imagery and tonality of the Judaeo-Christian tradition.

Passage spirituality does not have a morbid attraction to or obsession about death. It simply realizes and accepts it as a necessary part of the process toward new life. That process is ongoing, cyclic, indeed, happens over and over again in the course of a lifetime and in the evolution of the cosmos. Life, death and new life are the nature of things. Passage spirituality became for me the reason to go on in my therapeutic process, in my struggle to grow. It remains the single most powerful motivating energy within me. Paul wrote, "If we have died with Christ, we believe we are also to live with him." All struggles become worthwhile if seen and experienced in the context of death and resurrection. That passage —from self-centeredness to other-centeredness, from sin to grace, from emotional turbulence to peace—is a passage shared in consciousness with the dying-rising Jesus and the dying-rising world around us.

Death, death, and death

Passage spirituality necessitates the facing and feeling about, three different types of death. Those three very real types of death are threshold experiences for surrendering more profoundly to the love and Spirit of God. They are avenues or passageways to growth or new life. The most obvious form of death we need to face is *ultimate death*, the termination of physical existence. Ultimate death is the bottom line issue of our own physical existence, and the bottom line issue in our relating to those whom we love. Death reminds us of the existential lack of control that we have over our own lives and the lives of the people that we love. That lack of control can be denied, resisted, or become the springboard for deeper trust in and surrender to God's love.

Our struggle with ultimate death is echoed in two other forms of death that we face regularly. One I refer to as "deaths that happen." I referred to this type of experience earlier under the category of "life accidents." This category of life experiences includes disappointments, rejections, failures, losses, sickness and on and on. "Deaths that happen" are the bumps on the road of life—some rather significant, others not so significant—that surprise us or cause us pain. As with ultimate death, these experiences need to be approached with paschal, or passage spirituality. The new life that often is experienced in hindsight, after the experience, can consist of new learning, a changed emotional response to life, new courage for living, or a new approach to relationships.

"Deaths that are chosen" are a final category for our consideration. Paul wrote in Colossians 3:5: "Put to death whatever in your nature is rooted in earth . . . . " Resurrection is not only eternal life waiting for us on the other side of death. Neither is it the growth we experience through painful experiences that happen to us. Resurrection, or eternal life, is a new ethic or moral code. It involves our "putting to death" whatever that is within us that robs us or others of gospel peace and joy. Our traditional notions of mortification and asceticism have at their roots this spirituality of freely choosing the crucifixion of a part of ourselves that is obviously in need of grace and new life. Again, before one would even attempt this, there needs to be the Easter faith, the spiritual courage that motivates us to freely choose a Good Friday cross that we believe will result in Easter new life. For me, practicing paradoxical intention, paradoxical prayer, penetrating pseudo-guilt, not running from anxiety attacks, entering into . . . , listening, "lifting emotions up in prayer" —all became "chosen crosses, chosen deaths," avenues for my struggling passage spirituality to move toward new freedom and life.

A Synthesis on Death

The paschal mystery, therefore, can be experienced in a number of different ways. Entrance into paschal spirituality on any level—ultimate death, deaths that happen, or chosen deaths—prepares one for paschal experiences on other levels. My chosen deaths prepare me for deaths that happen. Deaths that happen, experienced in faith, are a kind of rehearsal for a faithful integration of my own ultimate death and the death of my loved ones.

In short, in the many different ways that one experiences death, there can be found the very core of the possibilities and opportunities for growth, new life, and resurrection. In the death moment, one can profoundly practice "Into Your Hands," or co-operative surrender spirituality. In the loss of control, we are released into the sway and influence of the Holy Spirit.

Reconciliation: A Way of Life

The rather highly developed Christology of John's gospel refers a number of times to God's glory. God's glory refers to the life of peace, joy, love, and full life which Jesus achieved for himself in the paschal event. It refers also to the share in that new life that Jesus offers to disciples as free gift. In Johannine thought, disciples experience the life of glory through faith, community, sacraments, and a relational bond with Jesus in which he becomes "home, dwelling place, the wine, bread, and new vision for us."

Life, for the anxious, the stress-filled, and the depressed is a progressive experience of and growth in this life of glory. Reconciliation is much more than a rote ritual for Saturday afternoons. Reconciliation, the step by step appropriation of glory and salvation, is the way of life for the disciple.

Jesus did not come that we might survive, but rather that we, as he did, might "passover" to fullness of life.

APPENDIX

Strategies for Establishing a Horizons Group

IN 1981, I began a group process entitled *Horizons* in several parishes around the Archdiocese of Chicago. I include a list of steps here for anyone who might be interested in starting similar faith-rooted self-help groups for the emotionally troubled. The group needs a group leader who is aware of the dynamics of neurosis and the healing of neurosis as described in this book. Horizons groups rather informally discuss the ideas and steps of spiritual healing presented in these pages and relate them to participants' stories. I include here several suggestions for people interested in such groups. Individuals who wish to systematically use the ideas from this book can adapt these suggestions for their own use.

1) A trained staff member should serve as a liaison to a Horizons group. This staff member, while not necessarily attending each meeting, trains para-professional leaders to lead and guide discussion.

2) Horizons is not intended for the severely troubled, for example those who have lost touch with reality or those suffering from addictions. The staff member responsible for the group, as well as the group leaders need to prayerfully and gently screen candidates.

3) Through advertising in local papers and parish bulletins and mailings, people of a given area should be informed that a ministry to the emotionally struggling is beginning.

4) At the first meeting, the trained staff member, should give an overview of the program. I recommend that the first session of Horizons last four to six weeks. In that period, this book is read week by week, and the group focuses attention on the theme of that particular section of the book.

5) Group meetings include reactions to or questions about the various themes (i.e., listening, paradoxical intention, developing a spiritual program), but then move to a sharing of participants' stories and struggles relative to the theme. The group leader(s), trained by the delegated staff member, keep the discussion flowing, focused, and well-timed.

6) Horizons meetings should last two to two-and-a-half hours, with time toward the middle for refreshments.

7) At the end of the initial weeks of community building and education, members can decide about the future: whether some want to continue in a support group. As with A.A., and other support groups, the group receives its direction by returning to the steps and attitudes contained in this book over and over again, and looking at participants' lives through the steps and attitudes.

8) If and when healing takes place in a participant's life, he or she should progress on to the next stage of helping someone else in emotional pain, either through a sponsoring relationship in the Horizons program, or facilitation of the group sessions.

9) The trained staff member need not be a trained counselor or therapist but should at least have up to date training in helping skills, group processing skills, knowledge of the neuroses, and pastoral ministry.